Mastering OCaml Programming

From Basics to Expert Proficiency

Contents

Introduction

OCaml is a powerful and expressive programming language belonging to the ML (Meta Language) family. With its roots in functional programming, OCaml has evolved to incorporate imperative and object-oriented paradigms, making it a versatile tool for various types of software development. The language offers a rich type system, type inference, pattern matching, and a robust module system, which together facilitate writing succinct, readable, and maintainable code.

This book is dedicated to providing a comprehensive guide to mastering OCaml programming. It targets both beginners and experienced programmers who wish to deepen their understanding of OCaml. The text begins with fundamental concepts, gradually building up to more advanced topics, ensuring that readers develop a solid foundation before tackling complex subjects.

One of the distinguishing features of OCaml is its type system. Unlike dynamically typed languages, OCaml performs type checking at compile-time, which helps catch errors early in the development process. This emphasis on type safety does not come at the expense of convenience; OCaml's type inference mechanism automatically deduces the types of expressions, allowing for concise code without sacrificing clarity or correctness.

In addition to the type system, OCaml's pattern matching capabilities offer a powerful way to deconstruct and analyze data structures. This feature is particularly useful for working with recursive data types such as lists and trees, enabling elegant and efficient solutions to a wide range of programming problems.

Functional programming is a core aspect of OCaml, promoting immutability and first-class functions. These paradigms encourage writing code that is less prone to side effects and easier to reason about.

However, OCaml does not restrict itself to functional programming. It seamlessly integrates imperative constructs, such as loops and mutable data structures, providing flexibility for developers who prefer an imperative approach.

OCaml's module system and functors offer advanced means of organizing and reusing code. Modules encapsulate related functions and types, promoting modularity and separation of concerns. Functors, which are functions that take modules as parameters and return new modules, allow for the creation of highly customizable and reusable components.

The OCaml ecosystem includes a wealth of libraries and tools that enhance the development experience. The OCaml top-level (REPL) provides an interactive environment for experimenting with code, while various build systems and package managers streamline the process of managing dependencies and building projects.

Throughout this book, we will explore these features in detail, starting with an introduction to the basic syntax and structure of OCaml programs. We will then delve into data types, control structures, functional programming, and data structures. Subsequent chapters will cover modules and functors, error handling, input and output, concurrency and parallelism, and advanced features and optimization techniques.

By the end of this book, readers will possess a thorough understanding of OCaml and be equipped to leverage its capabilities effectively in their own projects. Whether you are developing simple scripts, complex applications, or large-scale systems, mastering OCaml will provide you with the tools and knowledge to write efficient, reliable, and maintainable code.

We invite you to embark on this exploration of OCaml, where each chapter is designed to build upon previous knowledge, guiding you through the intricacies and nuances of the language. Let us now begin with the foundational concepts that will serve as the cornerstone for our journey into the world of OCaml programming.

Chapter 1

Introduction to OCaml

In this chapter, we will explore the foundational aspects of OCaml, including its installation and setup, basic syntax and structure, and the use of the OCaml top-level for interactive development. We will cover essential concepts such as variables, constants, and data types, and introduce key development tools and the language's type system. Additionally, we will provide guidance on writing and documenting OCaml code effectively, setting the stage for a deeper dive into OCaml programming.

1.1 What is OCaml?

OCaml, which stands for Objective Caml, is an industrial-strength programming language that melds functional, imperative, and object-oriented programming paradigms. This combination enables developers to take advantage of the different approaches for varying scenarios within a single consistent and powerful toolset. The core of OCaml is based on the Caml language, which has its roots in the ML family of programming languages, emphasizing type safety and functional programming.

The OCaml language offers a robust and expressive type system, which includes features like algebraic data types, pattern matching, and type inference. These features help in writing concise, safer code by catching errors at compile time, thus improving reliability and reducing runtime errors.

Functional Programming in OCaml allows developers to treat functions as first-class citizens, using higher-order functions and immutable data structures to create expressive and correct programs. Functional programming encourages the use of expressions and declarations rather than statements, promoting a style where the results of functions computations are returned and passed onward, rather than using mutable state.

Imperative Programming support in OCaml exists harmoniously alongside its functional aspects, providing familiar constructs such as loops, mutable variables, and input/output operations. These facilities enable developers to employ an imperative style when performance or simplicity dictates, without sacrificing the benefits of the language's type system.

Object-Oriented Programming in OCaml is facilitated through classes and objects, similar to languages like Java or C++. However, OCaml's object system is more flexible and allows optional typing of classes and methods, as well as multiple inheritance and structural subtyping. This capability can be particularly valuable when modeling complex data and behaviors.

OCaml's combination of these paradigms makes it particularly suitable for a wide range of applications, from financial systems and scientific computations to web services and systems programming. Let's illustrate some OCaml code snippets to ground our understanding.

A simple OCaml function:

```
let square x = x * x
```

This function is defined using the let keyword followed by the function name square, the parameter x, and the expression that produces the result. The let keyword is central in OCaml for binding values to variables or creating functions.

Executing this function in the OCaml top-level:

```
# let square x = x * x ;;
val square : int -> int = <fun>
# square 5 ;;
- : int = 25
```

The type system inferred the type of square as int -> int, indicating that it takes an integer and returns an integer. This type inference eliminates the need for explicit type annotations in many cases, making the code concise yet strongly typed.

OCaml also supports pattern matching, a powerful feature allowing the decomposition of data structures:

```
let describe_number x =
  match x with
  | 0 -> "zero"
  | 1 -> "one"
  | 2 -> "two"
  | _ -> "many"
```

Here, describe_number function provides descriptive strings for specific integers. The match...with construct evaluates the value of x, comparing it against the patterns. The underscore (_) is a wildcard pattern that matches any value not previously matched, ensuring all cases are handled.

OCaml's robust type system and pattern matching are particularly useful in combination with algebraic data types (ADTs), which allow developers to define complex data:

```
type shape =
  | Circle of float
  | Rectangle of float * float
```

This ADT defines a type shape that includes two variants: Circle and Rectangle. Each variant carries associated data – a radius for Circle, and width and height for Rectangle.

Functions can leverage pattern matching to operate on these types:

```
let area s =
  match s with
  | Circle r -> 3.14159 *. r *. r
  | Rectangle (w, h) -> w *. h
```

The area function computes the area of a shape by matching the input against the shape type and applying the appropriate formula. This method ensures that all cases are considered, providing compile-time checks that help avoid runtime errors.

OCaml's ecosystem offers a wide array of tools and libraries, further enhancing its productivity and usability. The language's sophisticated module system allows for encapsulation and separation of concerns, promoting modular and maintainable code. The supporting toolchain includes the OPAM package manager, the Dune build system, and various Integrated Development Environment (IDE) plugins, which facilitate smooth, efficient development workflows.

Let's summarize some defining attributes of OCaml: - Statically typed with powerful type inference. - First-class functions and emphasis on functional programming. - Support for imperative programming paradigms. - Comprehensive object-oriented features. - Extensive standard library and package ecosystem. - Strong support for modular and maintainable code development.

As we progress through this chapter, you will gain deep insights into how to leverage these features of OCaml to write elegant, efficient, and maintainable code.

1.2 Installation and Setup

To embark on your OCaml programming journey, the initial step is setting up the development environment. This entails installing OCaml and the associated tools necessary for efficient software development. This section provides detailed guidance on the installation process for various operating systems, ensuring a seamless setup regardless of the platform you are using.

Prerequisites:

- A working internet connection.
- Basic familiarity with command-line interfaces.

Installing OCaml

OCaml can be installed on different operating systems, including Linux, macOS, and Windows. Below we outline the steps for installing OCaml on these platforms.

Installing on Linux:

For Debian-based distributions such as Ubuntu, you can install OCaml using the package manager apt:

```
sudo apt-get update
sudo apt-get install ocaml ocaml-native-compilers camlp4-extra opam
```

For Red Hat-based distributions like Fedora, use dnf:

```
sudo dnf install ocaml ocaml-dune opam
```

Alternatively, for Arch Linux, you can use pacman:

```
sudo pacman -S ocaml opam
```

Installing on macOS:

The easiest way to install OCaml on macOS is by using Homebrew:

```
brew install ocaml opam
```

Installing on Windows:

For Windows, you can use the OCaml for Windows distribution which includes the OCaml compiler, OPAM, and other essential tools. Download the installer from https://fdopen.github.io/opam-repository-mingw/installation/ and follow the instructions provided on the website.

OPAM (OCaml Package Manager):

Regardless of your operating system, having OPAM (OCaml Package Manager) installed is crucial. It simplifies the management of OCaml versions and libraries. After installing OPAM, initialize it with the following command:

```
opam init
```

Follow the instructions that OPAM provides during initialization process. After initializing OPAM, it is recommended to install the latest OCaml version:

```
opam switch create 4.14.0 # Replace with the latest version number
eval $(opam env)
```

Verifying the Installation:

To ensure that OCaml and OPAM are installed correctly, you can check their versions:

```
ocamlc -version
opam --version
```

The output should resemble:

```
4.14.0
2.0.8
```

Setting up the OCaml Development Environment

Once OCaml and OPAM are installed, the next essential setup involves establishing a seamless development environment. Essential tools include an IDE or a text editor with OCaml support, and integration with version control systems like Git.

Text Editors and IDEs:

- VS Code: With the OCaml Platform extension, VS Code becomes a powerful tool tailored for OCaml development.

- Emacs: Emacs users can benefit from the tuareg mode, which provides advanced OCaml support.

- Vim: Installing the ocaml-language-server and configuring merlin enhances the OCaml development experience in Vim.

Here we show the installation steps for VS Code and the OCaml Platform:

- Download and install VS Code from https://code.visualstudio.com/.

- In VS Code, go to the Extensions view by clicking the Extensions icon in the Activity Bar on the side of the window or pressing Ctrl+Shift+X.

- Search for OCaml Platform and click Install.

Integrating Git:

To integrate Git for version control, ensure Git is installed on your machine:

```
sudo apt-get install git # For Debian-based systems
brew install git # For macOS
```

Configure your Git credentials:

```
git config --global user.name "Your Name"
git config --global user.email "Your Email"
```

Basic Git Commands:

Here are a few essential Git commands to familiarize yourself with:

```
git init # Initialize a new Git repository
git clone <repository_url> # Clone an existing repository
git add <file_name> # Stage changes
git commit -m "commit message" # Commit changes
git push # Push changes to remote repository
```

Ensuring a complete and robust development setup paves the way for a smoother OCaml programming experience. With the proper installation and environment configuration detailed above, you are now well-prepared to delve deeper into OCaml.

1.3 Hello, World! in OCaml

Creating a simple "Hello, World!" program in OCaml encapsulates the introductory concepts of the language. It allows users to familiarize themselves with OCaml's syntax, basic functions, and compilation/execution processes. This section offers a detailed understanding of how to write, compile, and execute a "Hello, World!" program in OCaml.

To begin, open your preferred text editor and create a new file named hello.ml. The extension .ml is used for OCaml source files. Add the following line of code in hello.ml:

```
print_endline "Hello, World!";;
```

In OCaml, print_endline is a function that outputs a string followed by a newline to the standard output. The double semicolon ;; is used to signal the end of the expression, which is particularly useful in the top-level or REPL (Read-Eval-Print Loop) environments.

To execute this program, two main approaches are available: using the OCaml top-level for an interactive experience or compiling the source file to create an executable.

Using the OCaml Top-Level

The OCaml top-level (also known as REPL) allows for quick testing and debugging of OCaml code. To run the hello.ml file in the top-level, follow these steps:

1. Navigate to the directory containing the hello.ml file. 2. Start the OCaml top-level by typing ocaml in your terminal.

This will present the OCaml interactive environment prompt:

```
        OCaml version 4.08.1
#
```

3. Load the file hello.ml using the #use directive:

```
# #use "hello.ml";;
```

The output should be:

```
Hello, World!
- : unit = ()
```

The text - : unit = () indicates that the expression has the type unit, which is OCaml's equivalent of void in other programming languages. It denotes that the expression is evaluated primarily for its side effects (in this case, printing to the console).

Compiling and Running the Program

For situations requiring standalone executables, OCaml provides a built-in compiler ocamlc. To compile and run the hello.ml file:

1. In the terminal, navigate to the directory containing the hello.ml file.
2. Compile hello.ml with ocamlc:

```
ocamlc -o hello hello.ml
```

Here, -o hello specifies the name of the output executable file. After compiling, an executable named hello is generated.

3. Run the executable:

```
./hello
```

The output will be:

```
Hello, World!
```

This basic exercise demonstrates file creation, usage of functions, and the compilation process in OCaml. It also serves the purpose of affirming the OCaml environment setup.

Exploring further, OCaml provides another approach to compilation via the ocamlopt compiler. The primary difference between ocamlc and ocamlopt lies in their compilation targets: ocamlc produces bytecode, while ocamlopt generates native code, producing more efficient executables.

To compile the hello.ml file using ocamlopt:

```
ocamlopt -o hello hello.ml
```

Run the resulting executable in the same manner:

```
./hello
```

The result will be:

```
Hello, World!
```

This section illustrates the fundamental steps for writing, compiling, and running a simple OCaml program, laying the groundwork for more sophisticated explorations. Careful attention to details such as correct file extensions, function usage, and compilation instructions ensures successful program execution.

1.4 Using the OCaml Top-Level

The OCaml top-level, also known as the OCaml REPL (Read-Eval-Print Loop), is an interactive environment where you can write and execute OCaml expressions and see their results immediately. It serves as an invaluable tool for learning the language, experimenting with code snippets, and rapid prototyping. To start the top-level, simply run the ocaml command in your terminal or command prompt:

```
$ ocaml
        OCaml version 4.12.0

$
```

Once the top-level is running, the # prompt appears, indicating that it is waiting for user input. You can now enter OCaml expressions and see the results instantaneously. For example:

```
# 1 + 2;;
- : int = 3
```

Here, $1 + 2$ is evaluated, returning 3, which is of type int.

Unlike many programming languages, OCaml requires that each statement in the top-level end with ;;. This syntax signifies the end of an expression, allowing the REPL to evaluate it. Omitting ;; at the end of an expression may result in the REPL waiting for additional input.

Let's delve into a few more examples to illustrate different features and functionalities of the OCaml top-level.

Defining Variables Variables in OCaml are defined using the let keyword. Here's how you can define and use a variable in the top-level:

```
# let x = 10;;
val x : int = 10

# x + 20;;
- : int = 30
```

In this example, x is defined as 10 and then used in an arithmetic operation. The top-level not only shows the result of the expression but also the type of the result.

Defining Functions Functions in OCaml are also defined using the let keyword. Here's an example of defining a simple function and using it:

```
# let add a b = a + b;;
val add : int -> int -> int = <fun>

# add 3 4;;
- : int = 7
```

The function add takes two integers and returns their sum. The top-level shows the type of the function, int -> int -> int, which means it takes two int values and returns an int.

Type Inference One of OCaml's strengths is its type inference capabilities. The top-level will automatically infer the types of expressions. Consider the following example:

```
# let square x = x *. x;;
val square : float -> float = <fun>

# square 2.5;;
- : float = 6.25
```

Here, the function square takes a float and returns a float. Note that the multiplication operator for floating-point numbers is *. instead of *.

Lists and Pattern Matching OCaml offers powerful list manipulation and pattern matching functionalities, which can be explored interactively in the top-level:

```
# let lst = [1; 2; 3; 4];;
val lst : int list = [1; 2; 3; 4]

# List.map (fun x -> x * 2) lst;;
- : int list = [2; 4; 6; 8]

# let rec sum_list l = match l with
  | [] -> 0
  | hd :: tl -> hd + sum_list tl;;
val sum_list : int list -> int = <fun>

# sum_list lst;;
- : int = 10
```

In this snippet, we first define a list named lst. We then use List.map to double each element in the list. Additionally, we define a recursive function sum_list that uses pattern matching to sum all elements in the list.

Handling Errors If an error occurs during the evaluation of an expression, the top-level will display an error message:

```
# 1 / 0;;
Exception: Division_by_zero.
```

In this case, attempting to divide by zero raises the Division_by_zero exception. The top-level helps diagnose and debug such errors effectively.

Using External Libraries You can also load external libraries or modules into the top-level using the #use directive. For example, to load a module from a file named math.ml, use:

```
# #use "math.ml";;
```

The #use directive reads and evaluates the contents of the specified file as if they were typed at the top-level prompt.

```
# #require "core.top";;
```

This command loads the core.top library, enhancing the environment with a plethora of useful functions and types provided by the Core library.

Documentation and Help While working in the top-level, you can access documentation for various functions and modules using the ocamlbrowser or the ocaml manual. Additionally, community resources and forums provide a wealth of knowledge for problem-solving and advanced queries.

Overall, mastering the OCaml top-level enhances your ability to test, debug, and understand code effectively. The interactive nature of the REPL shortens the feedback loop, enabling you to learn and explore OCaml more efficiently.

1.5 Basic Syntax and Structure

OCaml, short for Objective Caml, combines functional, imperative, and object-oriented programming concepts. Understanding its basic syntax and structure is crucial for effective programming in OCaml. This section provides a detailed examination of OCaml's fundamental syntax elements, including expressions, statements, and the structure of programs.

Variables and Constants: Variables in OCaml are immutable by default, meaning once a value is assigned, it cannot be changed. To define a variable, use the let keyword:

```
let x = 10
```

For mutable variables, use the ref keyword, providing a reference that can be updated:

```
let x = ref 10
x := 20 (* Changing the value of x to 20 *)
```

Constants are similarly declared with let, but their values should not be changed:

```
let pi = 3.14159
```

Basic Data Types: OCaml supports several fundamental data types, including integers, floating-point numbers, booleans, and strings. Type inference allows the compiler to deduce the type from the context, though explicit type annotations can be used for clarity:

```
let a : int = 10
let b : float = 20.5
let c : bool = true
let d : string = "Hello, OCaml!"
```

Expressions and Statements: Expressions in OCaml return a value and can include literals, variable names, and function applications:

```
let sum = 10 + 20
let greeting = "Hello" ^ ", World!"
```

Statements, including conditionals and loops, control the flow of the program:

```
if a > b then
  print_endline "a is greater than b"
else
  print_endline "b is greater than or equal to a"
```

Loop constructs include for and while. For example:

```
for i = 1 to 10 do
  print_endline (string_of_int i)
done

let count = ref 0 in
while !count < 10 do
```

```
  print_endline (string_of_int !count);
  incr count
done
```

Function Definitions: Functions are first-class citizens in OCaml and can be defined using the let keyword:

```
let add x y = x + y
```

Higher-order functions that take functions as arguments or return functions can also be defined:

```
let apply_twice f x = f (f x)
```

Anonymous functions (lambdas) are created using the fun keyword:

```
let increment = fun x -> x + 1
```

Tuples and Lists: Tuples group multiple values of potentially different types:

```
let tuple_example = (1, "OCaml", 3.14)
```

Lists are homogenous sequences of elements:

```
let numbers = [1; 2; 3; 4; 5]
```

List operations include the use of :: for prepending elements and @@ for concatenation:

```
let new_list = 0 :: numbers
let concatenated_list = new_list @ [6; 7]
```

Pattern Matching: Pattern matching is a powerful feature for deconstructing data types:

```
let rec factorial n =
  match n with
  | 0 -> 1
  | _ -> n * factorial (n - 1)
```

Pattern matching goes beyond integers, extending to tuples, lists, and custom data types.

Custom Data Types: Define custom data types using the type keyword. Sum types (variants) and product types (records) are commonly used.

Variants:

```
type color = Red | Green | Blue
```

```
let favorite_color = Red
```

Records:

```
type person = { name : string; age : int }
let john = { name = "John"; age = 30 }
```

Modules and Signatures: Modules group related definitions, promoting encapsulation and code organization. Define modules using the module keyword:

```
module Math = struct
  let add x y = x + y
  let sub x y = x - y
end
```

Access module members via the dot notation:

```
let result = Math.add 5 3
```

Signatures define the interface of a module:

```
module type MATH = sig
  val add : int -> int -> int
  val sub : int -> int -> int
end
```

Implement the signature using the : operator:

```
module Math : MATH = struct
  let add x y = x + y
  let sub x y = x - y
end
```

This comprehensive understanding of OCaml's basic syntax and structure forms the foundation for more advanced programming techniques, ensuring efficient and effective code development.

1.6 Comments and Documentation

Comments and documentation are crucial components in any programming language, and OCaml is no exception. Utilizing comments effectively can enhance code readability and maintainability, facilitate debugging, and serve as a guide for the developers who may work on the code in the future. In OCaml, comments are straightforward to use but powerful in their simplicity and utility.

Single-line Comments: In OCaml, single-line comments begin with (*

and end with *). They can be placed anywhere within the code and OCaml's compiler will ignore them. These are useful for short notes or explaining simple pieces of code.

```
(* This is a single-line comment in OCaml *)
let x = 42 (* This initializes x with the value 42 *)
```

Multi-line Comments: Multi-line comments in OCaml also start with (* and end with *), but can span multiple lines. They are helpful for providing more extensive explanations or commenting out large blocks of code during testing and debugging.

```
(* This is a multi-line comment in OCaml.
   It can span multiple lines and is very useful
   for providing detailed comments or documentation. *)
let y = x + 1
```

One important characteristic of OCaml comments is that they support nesting. This means you can place comments within comments, which comes in handy when you need to temporarily comment out code that already contains comments.

```
(* This is an outer comment.
   (* This is a nested comment inside the outer comment. *)
   The outer comment continues here. *)
let z = y + 2
```

Documentation Comments: OCaml also supports special comments for autogenerated documentation, known as documentation comments or docstrings. These are marked with (** ... *). The odoc tool can parse these special comments to generate API documentation.

```
(** This function adds two integers.
   @param a The first integer
   @param b The second integer
   @return The sum of a and b *)
let add a b =
  a + b
```

odoc uses a markup language for documentation comments, allowing you to include tags and annotations. Some common tags include:

- @param: Describes a parameter.
- @return: Describes the return value.
- @raise: Documents exceptions raised by the function.
- @see: References other functions or modules.

Inline Documentation: Good documentation practices not only involve comments but also extend to inline documentation within the code. This includes clear naming conventions for variables, functions, and modules, and the use of descriptive identifiers. This practice enhances code readability and self-documentation.

```
(** [factorial n] computes the factorial of [n].
    @param n A non-negative integer
    @return The factorial of [n]
    @raise Invalid_argument if [n] is negative. *)
let rec factorial n =
  if n < 0 then invalid_arg "n must be non-negative"
  else if n = 0 then 1
  else n * factorial (n - 1)
```

In this example, the function factorial is documented using a docstring that includes a description of the parameters, the return value, and the exception that may be raised. The clear naming and commenting, along with the documentation string, make it easy to understand the purpose and behavior of the function.

Tools for Documentation: Utilizing tools like odoc helps maintain high-quality documentation. odoc scans OCaml source files for docstrings, then generates HTML documentation that can be browsed and searched.

```
# To generate documentation using odoc
odoc compile --package my_package -o my_package.odoc my_module.cmt
odoc html --output-dir=docs my_package.odoc
```

Employing odoc ensures that the documentation is consistently formatted and provides an easy way to distribute and share documentation with other developers.

Creating comprehensive documentation using comments and tools like odoc not only improves code maintainability but also acts as a valuable resource for learning and reference, especially within collaborative environments.

1.7 OCaml Development Tools

Effective development in OCaml relies significantly on the use of a robust set of development tools. These tools facilitate various aspects of programming, including code editing, compilation, debugging, and project management. This section provides an in-depth overview of some of the most essential OCaml development tools, ensuring that programmers can optimize their productivity and maintain the quality of their code.

OPAM: OCaml Package Manager

OPAM (OCaml Package Manager) is the primary tool for managing OCaml libraries and extensions. It simplifies the installation, upgrading, and removal of packages, ensuring that dependencies are handled correctly.

```
$ opam init
$ opam switch create 4.12.0
$ eval $(opam env)
```

The commands above initialize OPAM, create a new switch (an isolated environment for OCaml development), and set up the environment for the newly created switch. OPAM allows multiple OCaml versions to coexist, making it easier to manage projects that require different compiler versions.

Dune: Build System

Dune is a popular build system for OCaml projects. It is designed to be fast, portable, and to handle complex dependency graphs efficiently. A basic Dune project requires a dune file to specify how the code should be built.

```
(executable
  (name my_program)
  (libraries core stdio))
```

In the example above, my_program is the name of the executable, and it depends on the core and stdio libraries. Dune automatically determines the build order, compiles the code, and links the executables.

To build the project, use the command:

```
$ dune build
```

Merlin: Code Assistance

Merlin is an OCaml language server that integrates with many popular editors, providing code completion, type inference, and error checking.

It enhances the development experience by offering real-time feedback and suggestions.

To install Merlin:

```
$ opam install merlin
```

For Vim users, Merlin can be integrated by adding the following to the .vimrc:

```
let g:opamshare = substitute(system('opam var share'),'\n$','','''')
execute "set rtp+=" . g:opamshare . "/merlin/vim"
```

Similarly, Emacs users can configure Merlin by adding the following to the init.el:

```
(let ((opam-share (substring (shell-command-to-string "opam var share 2> /dev/null")
      0 -1)))
  (add-to-list 'load-path (concat opam-share "/emacs/site-lisp"))
  (require 'merlin)
  (add-hook 'tuareg-mode-hook 'merlin-mode)
  (add-hook 'caml-mode-hook 'merlin-mode))
```

OCamlFormat: Code Formatting

Consistent code formatting is crucial for maintaining readability and collaboration in projects. OCamlFormat is a tool that automatically formats OCaml code according to a specified style.

Install OCamlFormat via OPAM:

```
$ opam install ocamlformat
```

To format a file:

```
$ ocamlformat my_file.ml
```

Including a .ocamlformat file in the project root allows customization of various formatting options, such as line length and indentation.

```
version=0.20
profile=conventional
```

OCaml-LSP: Language Server Protocol

OCaml-LSP (OCaml Language Server Protocol) facilitates improved integration with modern editors like VS Code and Atom. It provides advanced features like go-to-definition, find references, and more.

Installation is straightforward:

```
$ opam install ocaml-lsp-server
```

For VS Code users, the OCaml Platform extension can be installed from the VS Code marketplace, which seamlessly integrates OCaml-LSP.

OCaml Debugger

The OCaml debugger (ocamldebug) assists in diagnosing and fixing issues within OCaml programs. It supports setting breakpoints, stepping through code, and examining variable states.

To compile a program with debug information, use the -g flag:

```
$ ocamlc -g -o my_program my_program.ml
```

Then, start the debugger:

```
$ ocamldebug my_program
```

Within the debugger, common commands include:

```
break my_function        # Set a breakpoint at my_function
run                   # Run the program
step                  # Step to the next instruction
print x               # Print the value of variable x
```

OCaml Documentation: odoc

Documentation is essential for understanding and maintaining code. The odoc tool generates HTML documentation from OCaml source files, providing comprehensive and navigable documentation for projects.

Install odoc:

```
$ opam install odoc
```

To generate documentation:

```
$ odoc compile -I _build/default my_module.cmt
$ odoc html -I _build/default my_module.odoc
```

The generated HTML can be viewed in any web browser, facilitating easy access to detailed module descriptions, type information, and function signatures.

This collection of OCaml development tools enhances various stages of the programming lifecycle, from initial setup and code editing to debugging and documentation, ensuring a robust and efficient development experience.

1.8 Understanding OCaml's Type System

OCaml is statically typed, which means that the type of every expression is known at compile-time. This characteristic leads to enhanced reliability and performance of OCaml programs. The OCaml type system is both expressive and robust, allowing for powerful type inference, polymorphism, and type safety. Here we will delve into the key components and functionalities of the OCaml type system.

To begin, consider the following basic types available in OCaml:

- int – Represents integers.
- float – Represents floating-point numbers.
- bool – Represents Boolean values: true and false.
- char – Represents characters.
- string – Represents strings of characters.
- unit – Represents the unit type, which is similar to void in other languages, with a single value ().

In OCaml, the type of an expression can often be inferred automatically by the compiler based on the context in which it is used. This type inference system is a significant feature that allows for concise and readable code without the need for explicit type annotations. Consider the following example:

```
let a = 42
let b = 3.14
let c = "Hello, World!"
let d = true
```

Here, the type of a is inferred as int, b as float, c as string, and d as bool. The OCaml compiler uses the values assigned to these variables to infer their types.

However, explicit type annotations can also be provided if desired, using the : operator:

```
let e: int = 10
let f: float = 2.71
let g: bool = false
let h: string = "Type Annotations"
```

Beyond these basic types, OCaml also supports complex data types:

- tuples – Group multiple values of potentially different types into a single compound value. For example:

  ```
  let t = (1, "hello", 3.5)
  ```

- lists – Homogeneous collections of elements. For example:

  ```
  let l = [1; 2; 3; 4]
  ```

  Here, l is of type int_list.

Another cornerstone of OCaml's type system is algebraic data types (ADTs), which include:

- variant types – Define a type by enumerating its possible values. For instance:

  ```
  type color = Red | Green | Blue
  ```

  Here, color is a new type with three possible values: Red, Green, and Blue.

- record types – Similar to tuples, but with named fields. For example:

  ```
  type person = { name: string; age: int }
  let john = { name = "John"; age = 30 }
  ```

  Here, person is a record type with two fields: name and age.

Moreover, OCaml supports parametric polymorphism through type variables, enabling the definition of generic types. A classic example is the definition of a polymorphic list type:

```
type 'a my_list = Nil | Cons of 'a * 'a my_list
```

This defines a my_list type that can hold elements of any type, denoted by the type variable 'a.

```
Data: A polymorphic list 'a my_list
Result: Length of the list
Function length(lst):
    Data: Accumulator function for length calculation
    Function aux_len:
        lst acc
    if lst == Nil then
        return acc;
    else
        Data: Recursively call aux_len with tail of the list
        aux_len(lst_tail(lst), acc + 1);
    aux_len(lst, 0);
```

Understanding recursive data types and functions is essential due to the foundational role they play in functional programming, a paradigm strongly endorsed by OCaml.

Another critical aspect is the OCaml module system, which facilitates the encapsulation and abstraction of types and functions. Modules can contain types, which can then be more complex than the built-in types mentioned earlier:

```
module MyModule = struct
  type t = { x: int; y: int }
  let create x y = { x; y }
end
let p = MyModule.create 3 4
```

Higher-order types (or higher-kinded types), while not natively supported in OCaml, can often be simulated using techniques such as functors. Functors are module-level constructs that allow for the parametrization of modules over other modules:

```
module type Stack = sig
  type 'a t
  val create: unit -> 'a t
  val push: 'a -> 'a t -> 'a t
  val pop: 'a t -> 'a t
end

module ListStack: Stack = struct
  type 'a t = 'a list
  let create () = []
  let push x stack = x :: stack
  let pop = function
    | [] -> failwith "Empty stack"
    | _ :: tl -> tl
end
```

The OCaml type system is designed to provide powerful tools for creating robust and type-safe code. The combination of type inference, algebraic data types, parametric polymorphism, and a rich module system equips developers with a versatile and secure coding environment.

Chapter 2

Basic Data Types and Operators

This chapter delves into the fundamental building blocks of OCaml, covering primitive data types, variables, and constants. We will examine arithmetic and boolean operators, string manipulation, and the construction and usage of tuples and records. The chapter also offers insights into lists and arrays, and explains pattern matching along with type annotations and aliases, laying a robust foundation for understanding and working with data in OCaml.

2.1 Primitive Data Types

Understanding primitive data types is essential for effective OCaml programming. OCaml supports several built-in basic data types, each with specific properties and use cases. The core primitive data types in OCaml include int, float, bool, char, and string. We will explore each type in detail and examine how they can be used in programs.

Integer (int): The int type in OCaml represents whole numbers, both positive and negative. Integers are 31-bit values on 32-bit systems and 63-bit values on 64-bit systems. This allows for efficient arithmetic operations. Example declarations and initializations are as follows:

```
let x : int = 10;;
```

```
let y = -5;; (* Type inference applied *)
```

Integer operations include addition, subtraction, multiplication, division, and modulus, using the standard operators +, -, *, /, and mod.

```
let sum = x + y;;
let difference = x - y;;
let product = x * y;;
let quotient = x / y;;
let remainder = x mod y;;
```

Floating-point Numbers (float): The float type in OCaml is used for representing real numbers, containing both decimal and exponential components. Floats can store a much larger range of values compared to integers, but at the cost of precision. Declare float values using a period suffix:

```
let pi : float = 3.14159265358979;;
let e = 2.71828;; (* Type inference applied *)
```

Common operations on float values use the following operators: +., -. , *. , /., **. Note that float arithmetic operators are different from integer arithmetic operators.

```
let sum = pi +. e;;
let difference = pi -. e;;
let product = pi *. e;;
let quotient = pi /. e;;
let power = pi ** 2.0;;
```

Boolean (bool): The bool type encapsulates logical values, either true or false. Booleans are often used in control flow for conditional statements.

```
let is_valid : bool = true;;
let flag = false;; (* Type inference applied *)
```

Boolean operations include logical and (&&), logical or (||), and logical not (not).

```
let result = is_valid && flag;;
let alternative = is_valid || flag;;
let negation = not is_valid;;
```

Character (char): The char type is used to represent individual characters. Characters are denoted by single quotes.

```
let letter_a : char = 'a';;
let letter_b = 'b';; (* Type inference applied *)
```

Characters in OCaml can be manipulated using functions from the Char module:

```
let uppercase_a = Char.uppercase_ascii letter_a;;
let lowercase_b = Char.lowercase_ascii letter_b;;
```

String (string): The string type represents sequences of characters. Strings are denoted by double quotes.

```
let greeting : string = "Hello, OCaml!";;
let farewell = "Goodbye!";; (* Type inference applied *)
```

Strings in OCaml are immutable, and various operations like concatenation, slicing, and length measurement can be performed on them.

```
let message = greeting ^ " " ^ farewell;; (* Concatenation *)
let sub_greeting = String.sub greeting 0 5;; (* Slicing *)
let message_length = String.length message;; (* Length *)
```

Each primitive data type in OCaml is optimized for different computational tasks, and understanding their distinct properties and operations is crucial for writing efficient and effective code. The decision of which data type to use typically depends on the specific requirements of the problem being solved, such as the need for precision, the range of values, and memory efficiency. Proper utilization of these types forms the foundation for developing robust OCaml applications.

2.2 Variables and Constants

In OCaml, variables and constants are essential constructs for storing and manipulating data. A *variable* is a named storage location that can hold different values at different times, while a *constant* is a named entity whose value does not change once it has been defined. This section explores the syntax, scope, and usage of variables and constants in OCaml, providing detailed examples to ensure clear understanding.

To declare a variable in OCaml, the let keyword is used. The basic syntax is as follows:

```
let variable_name = expression;;
```

Here, variable_name is assigned the value resulting from the expression. OCaml uses type inference to determine the type of the variable based on the expression provided.

```
let x = 5;;
```

```
let y = x + 3;;
let message = "Hello, World!";;
```

The above example assigns the integer value 5 to the variable x, the result of x + 3 (which is 8) to the variable y, and the string "Hello, World!" to the variable message. Notice the use of ;; at the end of each line, which is necessary to mark the end of a statement in the OCaml interpreter.

Variables in OCaml are immutable by default, meaning that once a value has been assigned to a variable, it cannot be changed. To illustrate:

```
let x = 10;;
x = 20;; (* This will result in an error *)
```

Trying to reassign a value to x will result in an error as OCaml enforces immutability for variables declared with let. However, if mutability is required, you can use the ref keyword and the associated functions ! (dereferencing operator) and := (assignment operator).

```
let x = ref 10;;
x := 20;;
let y = !x + 5;;
```

In this example, x is defined as a reference to the integer 10, allowing its value to change. The statement x := 20 updates the value of x to 20. The dereferencing operator ! is used to access the current value of x, which is then used in the expression to define y.

Constants in OCaml are defined similarly to variables but, by definition, they are not meant to change after their initial assignment. To promote immutability, it is a common practice to define constant values using the let keyword.

```
let pi = 3.14159;;
let max_users = 100;;
```

In this code, pi and max_users are constants holding the values 3.14159 and 100, respectively. Although technically possible to reassign new values to these constants since they are declared using let, the naming convention suggests they should indeed be treated as constants.

Scope and shadowing are important aspects to consider in variable declaration. The scope of a variable is the region of the code within which the variable can be accessed. In OCaml, a variable's scope is limited to the block in which it is declared.

```
let x = 5;;
let f () =
    let x = 10 in
    x + 1;;
let result = f ();;
```

In this example, the function f has its own scope. Within the function, x is assigned the value 10, which shadows the outer x that holds the value 5. Inside f, x refers to the inner variable. Outside the function, result will be 11.

This concept of shadowing allows for flexibility in using variable names without redefining the outer scope variables. However, it is essential to exercise caution to avoid confusion and maintain code readability.

Variables and constants form the backbone of any OCaml program, enabling data storage and manipulation. The immutable nature of OCaml's let-bound variables leads to safer and more predictable code, while the ref keyword can be used for mutable state when necessary.

2.3 Arithmetic Operators

Arithmetic operations are fundamental in any programming language, and OCaml is no exception. In OCaml, these operations are defined for various primitive data types, especially integers and floating-point numbers. The language supports the standard arithmetic operators, including addition, subtraction, multiplication, division, modulo, and exponentiation. This section provides a detailed examination of each operator, highlighting their usage and any nuances specific to OCaml.

OCaml distinguishes between integer and floating-point arithmetic to maintain type safety and ensure precision in computations. This distinction is crucial as it affects the operator syntax used for different data types.

The primary arithmetic operators for integers (int types) in OCaml are: - Addition: + - Subtraction: - - Multiplication: * - Division: / - Modulo: mod

These operators are straightforward and work similarly to other procedural and functional programming languages. Here are some examples demonstrating their usage:

```
let a = 10;;
let b = 3;;
```

```
(* Addition *)
let c = a + b;; (* c is 13 *)

(* Subtraction *)
let d = a - b;; (* d is 7 *)

(* Multiplication *)
let e = a * b;; (* e is 30 *)

(* Division *)
let f = a / b;; (* f is 3 *)

(* Modulo *)
let g = a mod b;; (* g is 1 *)
```

It is important to note that the division operator (/) in the context of integers performs integer division. This means that the result of the division is truncated towards zero. For instance, in the given example, 10 / 3 is 3, discarding the remainder.

For arithmetic operations involving floating-point numbers (float types), OCaml uses different operators: - Addition: +. - Subtraction: -. - Multiplication: *. - Division: /.

These operators highlight the prevalent OCaml convention where floating-point operations are denoted with a suffix period (.) to distinguish them from integer operations. Here is an illustration of their usage:

```
let x = 10.0;;
let y = 3.0;;

(* Floating-point Addition *)
let z = x +. y;; (* z is 13.0 *)

(* Floating-point Subtraction *)
let w = x -. y;; (* w is 7.0 *)

(* Floating-point Multiplication *)
let u = x *. y;; (* u is 30.0 *)

(* Floating-point Division *)
let v = x /. y;; (* v is approximately 3.3333 *)
```

The floating-point division yields a precise result, preserving the fractional part, unlike integer division. This precision is critical in applications requiring accurate decimal computations, such as scientific calculations and financial modeling.

OCaml also supports the exponentiation operation for floating-point numbers using the ** operator:

```
let base = 2.0;;
let exponent = 3.0;;
```

```
(* Exponentiation *)
let result = base ** exponent;; (* result is 8.0 *)
```

It should be noted that there is no built-in operator for exponentiation for integer types in OCaml. Instead, one has to use the Pervasives module or define a custom function for integer exponentiation. Here is an example using a simple recursive function to achieve this:

```
let rec int_pow base exp =
  if exp = 0 then 1
  else base * int_pow base (exp - 1);;

(* Usage *)
let result = int_pow 2 3;; (* result is 8 *)
```

This custom function involves a recursive approach, decrementing the exponent until it reaches zero, at which point the function returns 1. The recursive calls multiply the base with itself exp times, simulating the behavior of exponentiation.

Understanding and utilizing these arithmetic operators is essential for performing computational tasks in OCaml. Their proper application ensures accurate and efficient arithmetic operations, forming the basis for more complex algorithms and functionalities in OCaml programming.

2.4 Boolean Operations

Boolean operations are fundamental in OCaml, as they are in many programming languages, enabling logical conditions and control flow mechanisms. At its core, the type bool in OCaml can assume one of two values: true or false. Boolean operations operate on these bool values to perform logical conjunctions, disjunctions, and negations.

OCaml supports the following basic Boolean operators:

- not: This unary operator computes the logical negation of a Boolean expression.
- &&: This binary operator computes the logical conjunction (AND) of two Boolean expressions.
- ||: This binary operator computes the logical disjunction (OR) of two Boolean expressions.

Understanding these operators requires examining their behavior through examples.

```
let a = true;;
let b = false;;

let negation = not a;;
let conjunction = a && b;;
let disjunction = a || b;;

print_endline (string_of_bool negation);;
print_endline (string_of_bool conjunction);;
print_endline (string_of_bool disjunction);;
```

Executing the above code results in:

```
false
false
true
```

The not operator reverses the value of its operand; hence not a results in false. The && operator requires both operands to be true for the result to be true, and a && b evaluates to false because b is false. On the other hand, the || operator produces true if at least one operand is true, making a || b evaluate to true.

Short-circuit evaluation is a significant feature of && and || operators. In a && b, if a evaluates to false, b is not evaluated, as the result is already determined to be false. Similarly, in a || b, if a is true, b is not evaluated because the result is guaranteed to be true. This ensures efficiency and can be critical in avoiding unnecessary or potentially harmful operations.

```
let safe_divide x y =
  y <> 0 && (x / y > 1);;

let result_true = safe_divide 10 2;;
let result_false = safe_divide 10 0;;

print_endline (string_of_bool result_true);;
print_endline (string_of_bool result_false);;
```

Execution yields:

```
true
false
```

The function safe_divide demonstrates short-circuit evaluation. Initially, y <> 0 is tested. If y is zero, the expression (x / y > 1) is not evaluated, preventing a division by zero error.

Boolean operations also enable more complex logical evaluations through combinators. Consider the following example illustrating multiple conditions using these logical operators:

```
let is_even x = x mod 2 = 0;;
let is_positive x = x > 0;;

let evaluate x =
    if is_even x && is_positive x then
        "Even and Positive"
    else if not is_even x && is_positive x then
        "Odd and Positive"
    else if is_even x && not (is_positive x) then
        "Even and Non-positive"
    else
        "Odd and Non-positive";;

let test_values = [2; -4; 3; 0];;
List.iter (fun x -> print_endline (evaluate x)) test_values;;
```

Execution yields:

```
Even and Positive
Even and Non-positive
Odd and Positive
Even and Non-positive
```

Here, the function evaluate determines the category of a number based on its parity (even or odd) and sign (positive or non-positive). This example leverages Boolean logic to create compound conditions, demonstrating how these operations form the backbone of decision-making in OCaml programs.

Understanding and effectively using Boolean operations are crucial for controlling program flow, validating conditions, and implementing algorithms that rely on logical conditions. Mastery of these concepts ensures robust, efficient, and error-free programming practices in OCaml.

2.5 String Manipulation

String manipulation is a fundamental aspect of programming in OCaml. Strings in OCaml are immutable sequences of characters, which means once a string is created, it cannot be modified. This immutability offers several benefits, such as thread safety and the ability to share strings freely without copying.

String is the primary module in OCaml for handling string operations. It provides a multitude of functions to create, manipulate, and query strings.

- **Creating Strings**: Strings can be defined using double quotes.

For example:

```
let greeting = "Hello, world!";;
```

- **Concatenation**: The^ operator is used for concatenating two strings.

```
let full_greeting = greeting ^ " Welcome to OCaml.";;
```

- **Length**: The String.length function returns the number of characters in a string.

```
let length_of_greeting = String.length greeting;;
```

- **Accessing Characters**: The String.get function is used to access a specific character in a string by its index.

```
let first_char = String.get greeting 0;;
```

- **Substrings**: The String.sub function extracts a substring from a string. It takes three arguments: the original string, the starting index, and the length of the substring.

```
let hello_substring = String.sub greeting 0 5;;
```

- **Iteration**: The String.iter function allows you to iterate over each character in a string. It takes a function as an argument and applies it to each character.

```
String.iter (fun c -> print_char c; print_char ' ') greeting;;
```

Output:

```
H e l l o ,   w o r l d !
```

- **Searching**: Several functions are available to search within strings. String.contains checks if a character is present, and String.index finds the first occurrence of a character.

```
let contains_comma = String.contains greeting ',';;
let first_occur = String.index greeting 'o';;
```

- **Trimming**: The String.trim function removes whitespace from both ends of the string.

```
let padded_string = " OCaml ";;
let trimmed_string = String.trim padded_string;;
```

More complex string manipulation tasks can be handled using auxiliary modules such as Str for regular expressions. For example, matching and replacing patterns within strings can be performed using the Str module.

- **Regular Expressions**: The Str.global_replace function can substitute all occurrences of a pattern in a string.

```
#require "str";;
let sentence = "OCaml is great. OCaml is powerful.";;
let new_sentence = Str.global_replace (Str.regexp "OCaml") "F#" sentence;;
```

Output:

```
F# is great. F# is powerful.
```

Generally, string manipulations in OCaml can be optimized by using buffers when dealing with large or mutable sequences of characters. The Buffer module offers mutable strings which allow efficient building and manipulation.

- **Using Buffers**: Buffers provide a way to accumulate characters or strings. You can add characters or strings to a buffer using Buffer.add_char and Buffer.add_string, respectively, and convert the buffer to a string with Buffer.contents.

```
let buffer = Buffer.create 16;;
Buffer.add_string buffer "Hello, ";;
Buffer.add_string buffer "mutable ";;
Buffer.add_string buffer "world.";;
let result = Buffer.contents buffer;;
```

Output:

```
Hello, mutable world.
```

Strings in OCaml, although immutable, offer a rich set of functions for manipulation through the String module and complementary modules such as Str and Buffer. These functionalities provide significant flexibility and power in managing and transforming text, enabling complex programming tasks to be performed efficiently and elegantly.

2.6 Tuples and Records

Tuples and records are composite data structures in OCaml that allow grouping of values. They are instrumental for structuring data in a more organized way compared to primitive data types.

Tuples in OCaml are fixed-size, heterogeneous collections of items. Each element in a tuple can have a different type, and these elements are collectively grouped together using parentheses. Here's an example of creating and manipulating a tuple:

```
let my_tuple = (1, "hello", 3.14)

let first_element = fst my_tuple (* Retrieves the first element *)
let last_element = snd my_tuple (* Retrieves the second element; for a two-tuple *)
```

To access tuple elements beyond the second item, pattern matching is utilized. Here's how you access elements in a three-tuple:

```
let (x, y, z) = my_tuple (* Pattern matching to extract values *)
```

It is crucial to note that tuples are best for small fixed collections of values. When the size of the collection is larger or needs more descriptive labeling, records are preferred.

Records in OCaml are collections of fields, each with a name and a value. They allow for better-managed complex data in a more readable and meaningful format by using labeled fields. Here's a basic record definition and initialization example:

```
type person = {
  name: string;
  age: int;
  email: string;
}

let john = {
  name = "John Doe";
  age = 30;
  email = "john@example.com"
}
```

Accessing fields within a record is straightforward using the dot notation:

```
let johns_age = john.age
let johns_email = john.email
```

Records in OCaml also support mutable fields, although immutability by default simplifies reasoning about and maintainability of code. Below is an example of a record with a mutable field:

```
type mutable_person = {
  name: string;
  mutable age: int;
}
```

```
let jane = {
  name = "Jane Doe";
  age = 25
}

jane.age <- 26 (* Changing the value of a mutable field *)
```

Pattern matching similarly extends to records, which facilitates extracting field values concurrently. Here is an example involving pattern matching with records:

```
let {name; age; email} = john (* Direct extraction of field values through pattern
    matching *)
```

The creation and manipulation of nested records are another powerful feature. For instance:

```
type address = {
  street: string;
  city: string;
}

type customer = {
  name: string;
  address: address;
}

let alice = {
  name = "Alice Smith";
  address = {
    street = "123 Maple St";
    city = "Wonderland"
  }
}

let alice_city = alice.address.city
```

When working with records, especially with many fields, updating a record without mutation is efficiently done using the *with* keyword, which facilitates creating a new record with some updated fields:

```
let updated_alice = { alice with city = "New Wonderland" }
```

Records can also leverage type inference for fields, ensuring type safety and reducing boilerplate code. Here, constructors and update syntax help maintain clean, understandable code while handling complex data structures in a scalable manner.

Combining tuples and records in OCaml allows for flexible, well-organized, and type-safe programming practices. Their usages range from efficiently handling small collections of elements using tuples to managing more complex and descriptive groupings with records, providing a robust foundation for building applications and abstracting data efficiently in OCaml.

2.7 Lists and Arrays

In OCaml, both lists and arrays are fundamental data structures that allow the storage and manipulation of collections of elements. Understanding the differences and use cases for each is crucial for effective OCaml programming.

Lists

A list in OCaml is an immutable sequence of elements of the same type. Lists are constructed using square brackets with elements separated by semicolons. The empty list is represented by [].

```
(* A list of integers *)
let int_list = [1; 2; 3; 4; 5]

(* An empty list *)
let empty_list = []
```

Constructing Lists

Lists can be efficiently constructed using the cons operator (::), which prepends an element to the front of an existing list.

```
(* Using the cons operator to construct a list *)
let int_list = 1 :: (2 :: (3 :: (4 :: (5 :: []))))
```

The cons operator builds the list from the rightmost element to the leftmost, making it suitable for recursive list construction.

List Operations

OCaml provides various built-in functions to operate on lists.

```
(* Getting the head and tail of a list *)
let head = List.hd int_list (* Returns 1 *)
let tail = List.tl int_list (* Returns [2; 3; 4; 5] *)

(* Checking if a list is empty *)
let is_empty = List.length empty_list = 0

(* Appending two lists *)
let appended_list = List.append int_list [6; 7; 8]
```

Pattern Matching with Lists

Pattern matching is a powerful feature used to decompose lists.

```
(* Pattern matching on lists *)
let rec sum lst = match lst with
  | [] -> 0
  | head :: tail -> head + sum tail

let total = sum int_list (* Returns 15 *)
```

Higher-Order Functions

OCaml supports higher-order functions, such as List.map, List.filter, and List.fold_left.

```
(* Applying a function to each element *)
let doubled_list = List.map (fun x -> x * 2) int_list (* Returns [2; 4; 6; 8; 10] *)

(* Filtering a list *)
let even_list = List.filter (fun x -> x mod 2 = 0) int_list (* Returns [2; 4] *)

(* Folding (reducing) a list *)
let sum = List.fold_left (+) 0 int_list (* Returns 15 *)
```

Arrays

An array is a mutable sequence of elements, all of the same type, and provides fast random access to its elements. Array elements are enclosed within square brackets and separated by semicolons.

```
(* An array of integers *)
let int_array = [|1; 2; 3; 4; 5|]

(* An empty array *)
let empty_array = [||]
```

Accessing and Modifying Arrays

Elements in an array can be accessed and modified using index notation.

```
(* Accessing elements *)
let second_element = int_array.(1) (* Returns 2 *)

(* Modifying elements *)
int_array.(1) <- 10
let modified_array = int_array (* Now [|1; 10; 3; 4; 5|] *)
```

Array Operations

OCaml's standard library provides numerous functions for operating on arrays.

```
(* Getting the length of an array *)
let length = Array.length int_array (* Returns 5 *)
```

```
(* Creating an array from a list *)
let array_from_list = Array.of_list int_list (* [|1; 2; 3; 4; 5|] *)

(* Converting an array to a list *)
let list_from_array = Array.to_list int_array (* [1; 10; 3; 4; 5] *)

(* Iterating over arrays with a function *)
Array.iter (fun x -> Printf.printf "%d " x) int_array
```

Higher-Order Functions with Arrays

Just as with lists, OCaml provides higher-order functions like Array.map and Array.fold_left for arrays.

```
(* Applying a function to each element *)
let doubled_array = Array.map (fun x -> x * 2) int_array (* [|2; 20; 6; 8; 10|] *)

(* Folding (reducing) an array *)
let sum_array = Array.fold_left (+) 0 int_array (* Returns 23 *)
```

While lists are ideal for scenarios where immutability and recursive processing are advantageous, arrays are preferred when direct access to elements and in-place modifications are necessary. Understanding the strengths and appropriate usage of each structure enables more effective OCaml programming.

2.8 Pattern Matching

Pattern matching in OCaml is a powerful mechanism that allows you to check a value against a pattern and to deconstruct data structures systematically and efficiently. It is a central feature in OCaml due to its highly expressive nature and its ability to succinctly handle various data types and structures. Pattern matching goes beyond simple equality checks, providing a clear and concise way to work with complex data types.

The match construct is the most common way to perform pattern matching in OCaml. The syntax of a match expression is as follows:

```
match expression with
| pattern1 -> result1
| pattern2 -> result2
| ...
| patternN -> resultN
```

Each pattern is checked in the order they are written until a match is found. When a match is found, the corresponding result expression is evaluated. Let us consider an example using an integer:

```
let evaluate_number n =
  match n with
  | 0 -> "zero"
  | 1 -> "one"
  | _ -> "other"
```

Here, evaluate_number takes an integer n and matches it against three patterns: 0, 1, and the wildcard pattern _ which matches any value not previously matched.

Pattern matching can also be used to deconstruct data structures such as lists and tuples. For instance, consider the following function that sums the first two elements of a list:

```
let sum_first_two l =
  match l with
  | x :: y :: _ -> x + y
  | _ -> 0
```

In this example, the pattern x :: y :: _ matches a list with at least two elements and binds the first two elements to x and y, respectively. The wildcard pattern _ matches the rest of the list, which we ignore. If the list has fewer than two elements, the wildcard case handler returns 0.

Tuple deconstruction is another typical use case for pattern matching. Consider a function that swaps the first two elements of a tuple:

```
let swap (a, b) = (b, a)

let result = match (3, 4) with
  | (x, y) -> (y, x)
```

Here, the swap function and the match expression deconstruct the tuple into its individual components, a and b in the function, and x and y in the match expression respectively, performing the swap.

Pattern matching on records can be performed by specifying the fields in the record. Consider the following example:

```
type person = { name : string; age : int }

let is_adult p =
  match p with
  | { name = _; age = a } when a >= 18 -> true
  | _ -> false
```

In this example, is_adult takes a record of type person and matches it against a pattern with a conditional guard (using when). If the age field is 18 or more, the function returns true; otherwise, it returns false.

Nested pattern matching is employed when working with more complex data structures. Consider this example involving a tree data structure:

```
type tree =
  | Leaf
  | Node of int * tree * tree

let rec sum_tree t =
  match t with
  | Leaf -> 0
  | Node (v, left, right) -> v + (sum_tree left) + (sum_tree right)
```

The sum_tree function handles a binary tree, summing up all the integer values contained in the Nodes. The branch Leaf is the base case, returning 0. For a Node, the pattern (v, left, right) deconstructs the node into its value and its left and right subtrees, recursively summing the values.

Pattern matching is crucial when dealing with option types. Option types, often used to represent nullable values, can easily be handled with pattern matching:

```
let increment_option opt =
  match opt with
  | Some x -> Some (x + 1)
  | None -> None
```

This function increments the value inside an option if it exists (Some), returning None otherwise.

Patterns may incorporate wildcards, variable bindings, constants, algebraic data types, lists, tuples, records, and even other patterns, showcasing their versatility. Effective use of pattern matching improves code clarity and robustness, adhering to OCaml's functional programming paradigm and making it a powerful feature to master.

2.9 Type Annotations and Aliases

Type annotations in OCaml provide a clear and explicit way to define the types of variables, function parameters, and return values. This form of explicit typing can help with the readability and maintainability of the code, as well as with early detection of type-related errors. Aliases, on the other hand, offer a method to simplify complex type expressions, making it easier to manage and understand the code. In this section, we will explore how to use type annotations and aliases effectively.

Type Annotations

Type annotations can be added to variables, function parameters, and return types. The syntax for annotating a type is to follow the variable or expression with a colon (:) and the type.

Variable Annotations

To annotate the type of a variable, place the annotation directly after the variable name.

```
let x: int = 7;;
let message: string = "Hello, OCaml!";;
```

Here, x is explicitly annotated as an int, and message is annotated as a string.

Function Annotations

For functions, types can be annotated for both parameters and return values. The type of each parameter is enclosed in parentheses, and the return type follows the arrow (→).

```
let add (a: int) (b: int): int = a + b;;
let concat_strings (s1: string) (s2: string): string = s1 ^ s2;;
```

In the add function, both parameters a and b are annotated as int, and the return type is also an int. The concat_strings function has string annotations for its parameters and return type.

Complex Types

OCaml supports complex types such as lists, tuples, and records. Type annotations can also be applied to these complex types.

```
let int_list: int list = [1; 2; 3; 4; 5];;
let string_tuple: (string * string) = ("OCaml", "Programming");;
let student_record: {name: string; age: int} = {name = "Alice"; age = 20};;
```

In these examples, int_list is annotated as a list of integers, string_-tuple as a tuple of two strings, and student_record as a record with name and age fields.

Type Aliases

Type aliases provide a way to create synonymous names for existing types. This can simplify the usage of complex types and improve code readability. Type aliases are defined using the type keyword.

Basic Type Aliases

To create a basic type alias, use the following syntax:

```
type coordinates = float * float;;
let origin: coordinates = (0.0, 0.0);;
let point: coordinates = (1.5, 2.5);;
```

Here, coordinates is defined as an alias for a tuple of two floats. Now, coordinates can be used instead of float * float.

Record Type Aliases

Aliases can also be applied to record types. This allows the structured type to be reused more conveniently.

```
type student = {name: string; age: int; gpa: float};;
let alice: student = {name = "Alice"; age = 20; gpa = 3.8};;
let bob: student = {name = "Bob"; age = 22; gpa = 3.5};;
```

In this example, student is an alias for a record with three fields: name, age, and gpa. This alias makes it easier to create and manage records of this type.

Parameterized Type Aliases

OCaml supports parameterized type aliases, which are useful for creating generic types.

```
type 'a tree = Empty | Node of 'a * 'a tree * 'a tree;;

let rec insert x = function
    | Empty -> Node(x, Empty, Empty)
    | Node(y, left, right) ->
        if x < y then Node(y, insert x left, right)
        else Node(y, left, insert x right);;
```

Here, the 'a tree alias defines a binary tree type that can hold values of any type, indicated by the type variable 'a. The insert function demonstrates how this tree type can be used.

Employing type annotations and aliases in OCaml fosters not only a clear and maintainable codebase but also leverages the power of the type system to catch errors early in the development process.

Chapter 3

Control Structures

This chapter provides an in-depth look at OCaml's control structures, beginning with conditional statements and various loop constructs. We will delve into advanced pattern matching techniques and effective exception handling strategies. The use of Option and Result types for error management will be explored, along with the principles of recursive and higher-order functions. By combining these control structures, readers will learn how to write robust and efficient OCaml code.

3.1 Conditional Statements

OCaml provides a rich set of features for implementing conditional statements that allow us to control the flow of a program. Conditional statements facilitate the evaluation of expressions and decision-making based on the evaluation results. We will explore the two main conditional constructs available in OCaml: if-then-else statements and match-with expressions.

If-Then-Else Statement

The if-then-else statement is one of the fundamental control structures in OCaml. It evaluates a condition and executes the corresponding code block based on whether the condition is true or false. The syntax for the if-then-else statement is straightforward:

```
if condition then
  expression1
```

```
else
  expression2
```

Here, condition is a boolean expression that evaluates to true or false. If condition is true, expression1 is executed; otherwise, expression2 is executed.

For example, consider a simple program that determines if a number is positive, negative, or zero:

```
let determine_sign x =
  if x > 0 then
    "Positive"
  else if x < 0 then
    "Negative"
  else
    "Zero"
```

In this example, determine_sign evaluates the integer x. The first condition checks if x is greater than zero. If true, the function returns the string "Positive". If the first condition is false, the next if-then condition checks if x is less than zero. If true, the function returns "Negative". Otherwise, it returns "Zero".

Match-With Expression

The match-with expression is more powerful and flexible compared to the if-then-else statement. It allows for pattern matching against values, enabling a more expressive and concise way to handle different cases. The general syntax of match-with is:

```
match value with
| pattern1 -> expression1
| pattern2 -> expression2
| ...
| patternN -> expressionN
```

Each pattern is matched against the value. When a pattern matches, the corresponding expression is evaluated. If no patterns match, the program raises a Match_failure exception.

Consider the following example that determines the type of a given day:

```
type day = Monday | Tuesday | Wednesday | Thursday | Friday | Saturday | Sunday

let day_type d =
  match d with
  | Saturday | Sunday -> "Weekend"
  | Monday | Tuesday | Wednesday | Thursday | Friday -> "Weekday"
```

Here, day is a user-defined type representing days of the week. The day_type function uses match-with to classify days as either "Weekend" or "Weekday".

Combining If-Then-Else and Match-With

OCaml allows nested if-then-else and match-with expressions to handle complex conditional logic. For instance:

```
let analyze_number x =
  if x mod 2 = 0 then
    match x with
    | 0 -> "Zero"
    | _ -> "Even number"
  else
    "Odd number"
```

In the above code, analyze_number determines if x is an even number, odd number, or zero using a combination of if-then-else and match-with statements. If x mod 2 = 0, the match-case checks if x is zero or a non-zero even number. If the condition is false, it returns "Odd number".

Understanding and effectively using these conditional constructs is essential for writing robust and efficient OCaml programs. Leveraging the expressive power of if-then-else and match-with enables developers to implement complex decision-making logic accurately and concisely.

3.2 Loops in OCaml

In OCaml, loops enable iterative execution of code blocks. Unlike imperative languages, OCaml's preference for functional paradigms means looping is often achieved through recursion. However, for completeness, OCaml also supports traditional iteration constructs such as for and while loops. Understanding both recursion and these iterative constructs is crucial for proficient OCaml programming.

For Loops

The for loop in OCaml iterates over a range of integers. The general syntax is:

```
for i = start to end do
  (* body of the loop *)
done
```

Here, i is the loop variable that sequentially takes on each integer value from start to end. This range is inclusive on both ends. Use downto instead of to to decrement the loop variable:

```
for i = start downto end do
```

```
  (* body of the loop *)
done
```

Example: Calculating the Sum of First n Natural Numbers

Consider the following program that calculates the sum of the first n natural numbers.

```
let sum_natural n =
  let sum = ref 0 in
  for i = 1 to n do
    sum := !sum + i
  done;
  !sum
```

In this example, sum is a reference (a mutable variable) initialized to 0. The for loop iterates from 1 to n, updating sum with the current value of i. The dereference operator ! is used to access the reference value while := is used for assignment.

While Loops

The while loop iterates as long as its condition remains true. Its general syntax is:

```
while condition do
  (* body of the loop *)
done
```

Example: Finding the First Power of 2 Greater than a Given Number

Here is a program using a while loop to find the smallest power of 2 greater than a given number n.

```
let first_power_of_two_gt n =
  let power = ref 1 in
  while !power <= n do
    power := !power * 2
  done;
  !power
```

In this example, the loop condition !power <= n ensures that the loop continues multiplying power by 2 until it exceeds n.

Recursive Loops

Although for and while loops are available, OCaml's functional nature favors recursion for repeated tasks. Recursive functions are those that call themselves to perform their task iteratively. Recursion is implicitly tail-recursive in many functional languages, including OCaml, making it efficient for iterative computations when combined with the tailrec annotation.

Example: Factorial Calculation Using Recursion

The following code calculates the factorial of a number using recursion:

```
let rec factorial n =
  if n <= 1 then 1
  else n * factorial (n - 1)
```

factorial is a recursive function that multiplies n by the factorial of n-1 until n is 1 or less.

Example: Tail-Recursive Sum of a List

Tail-recursion is preferable for performance, as it ensures that the stack does not grow with each recursive call. Here is an example of a tail-recursive function to sum the elements of a list:

```
let sum_list lst =
  let rec aux lst acc =
    match lst with
    | [] -> acc
    | head :: tail -> aux tail (acc + head)
  in
  aux lst 0
```

The helper function aux carries an accumulator acc that holds the running sum. This accumulator ensures that the recursion is tail-recursive.

Handling Infinite Loops

Infinite loops are rare in functional programming but can be constructed intentionally using recursion or while loops. An infinite loop running indefinitely:

```
let rec infinite_loop () =
  print_endline "Running...";
  infinite_loop ()
```

The infinite_loop function prints "Running..." indefinitely as it calls itself recursively without a base case.

Iterative Constructs in Practice

Choosing between recursion and iteration depends on the problem at hand. Recursion is more idiomatic for functional query languages like OCaml but for and while are sometimes more intuitive. Understanding both paradigms is essential to writing clean, efficient, and idiomatic OCaml code.

This comprehensive understanding of iterative constructs and their practical applications equips you with the necessary tools to tackle a wide range of programming tasks efficiently and idiomatically in OCaml.

3.3 Pattern Matching in Depth

Pattern matching is a cornerstone of functional programming in OCaml, providing a powerful mechanism to destructure data and make code concise and readable. Pattern matching allows a program to inspect the structure of data types and execute code based on that structure. We will explore the various aspects of pattern matching, including its syntax, use cases, and performance considerations.

Basic Syntax: The simplest form of pattern matching is the match expression. This expression evaluates a value and matches it against a series of patterns, executing the code associated with the first matching pattern.

```
let describe_number x =
  match x with
  | 0 -> "zero"
  | 1 -> "one"
  | _ -> "other"
```

In this example, the function describe_number takes an integer x and returns a string describing x. The match expression evaluates x:

- If x is 0, the result is "zero".
- If x is 1, the result is "one".
- For any other value, the wildcard pattern _ matches, returning "other".

Pattern Components: Patterns can be more complex than simple constants or wildcards. Variables, constants, wildcards, tuples, lists, and algebraic data types can all be part of a pattern.

```
let rec sum_list lst =
  match lst with
  | [] -> 0
  | head :: tail -> head + sum_list tail
```

Here, sum_list computes the sum of a list. The pattern matching expression:

- []: Matches an empty list, returning 0.

- head :: tail: Matches a non-empty list, binding head to the first element and tail to the rest of the list. It recursively sums tail, adding head.

Pattern Matching with Algebraic Data Types: OCaml's pattern matching shines when dealing with algebraic data types. Consider a type representing a binary tree:

```
type binary_tree =
  | Leaf
  | Node of int * binary_tree * binary_tree

let rec sum_tree t =
  match t with
  | Leaf -> 0
  | Node (value, left, right) -> value + (sum_tree left) + (sum_tree right)
```

The binary_tree type can be either a Leaf or a Node that contains an integer value and two subtrees. In the sum_tree function, pattern matching:

- Leaf: Matches a leaf node, returning 0.
- Node (value, left, right): Matches a node, binding value, left, and right. It sums the values of the left and right subtrees, including the current node's value.

Destructuring Tuples: Pattern matching can also destructure tuples.

```
let add_pair p =
  match p with
  | (x, y) -> x + y
```

The add_pair function takes a tuple p and matches it with the pattern (x, y), binding x and y to the first and second elements of the tuple. The result is the sum of x and y.

Or Patterns and As Patterns: Pattern matching allows for multiple patterns to match the same branch using the | symbol (or patterns) and to use the as keyword to bind a sub-pattern.

```
let describe_even_odd n =
  match n with
  | 0 -> "zero"
  | 2 | 4 | 6 -> "an even small number"
  | 1 | 3 | 5 -> "an odd small number"
  | _ as m -> if m mod 2 = 0 then "even" else "odd"
```

Here, numbers 2, 4, and 6 are matched as "an even small number", and

1, 3, and 5 as "an odd small number". Any other number is matched by the wildcard pattern _, named m, which allows for further computation.

Pattern Matching with Lists: Using patterns to match specific list structures can simplify list operations.

```
let rec take n lst =
  match (n, lst) with
  | (0, _) -> []
  | (_, []) -> []
  | (n, head :: tail) -> head :: (take (n - 1) tail)
```

The function take retrieves the first n elements from a list. The patterns are:

- (0, _): Matches when n is 0, returning an empty list.
- (_, []): Matches when the list is empty, returning an empty list.
- (n, head :: tail): Matches when the list is non-empty, binding head and tail. It recursively calls take to fetch the next n-1 elements from tail, prepending head.

Guarded Patterns: Patterns can have conditions attached, known as when guards.

```
let classify_number n =
  match n with
  | n when n < 0 -> "negative"
  | 0 -> "zero"
  | n when n > 0 -> "positive"
```

The classify_number function uses guards to classify a number as "negative", "zero" or "positive".

Performance Considerations: Complex pattern matching can have performance implications. Since patterns are checked in order, minimising the number of checks and reordering patterns to match more frequent cases earlier can enhance performance. For deep recursive structures like lists and trees, ensure tail-recursion and avoid excessive backtracking.

OCaml's optimizing compiler efficiently handles many pattern matching constructs. However, for very complex or nested patterns, consider breaking them into separate functions or using direct conditional expressions to improve readability and performance.

Pattern matching in OCaml not only enhances the clarity and structure of the code but also enables robust and expressive handling of complex data types.

3.4 Exception Handling

Exception handling is a critical aspect of robust software development. In OCaml, handling exceptions effectively allows for the management of unexpected conditions and error states, ensuring that programs can respond gracefully to erroneous input or operational failures. This section covers the fundamental concepts of raising and handling exceptions in OCaml, with detailed examples showcasing their usage.

OCaml uses the exception keyword to define new exceptions, and the raise function to signal that an error has occurred. Exceptions can be caught and handled using the try...with construct.

To define a custom exception:

```
exception MyException of string
```

This defines an exception named MyException that carries a string payload. To raise this exception, use the raise function as follows:

```
let risk_function x =
  if x < 0 then
    raise (MyException "Negative value not allowed")
  else
    x * 2
```

In this example, the function risk_function doubles its input unless the input is negative. If the input is negative, MyException is raised with a descriptive message.

Handling exceptions involves the try...with construct:

```
let safe_function x =
  try
    risk_function x
  with
  | MyException msg ->
    print_endline ("Caught an exception: " ^ msg);
    -1
```

Here, safe_function calls risk_function. If risk_function raises MyException, the exception is caught, and a message is printed. The function then returns -1 as a fallback value.

The general form of a try...with expression is:

```
try
  (* code that may raise an exception *)
with
  | Exception1 -> handler1
  | Exception2 -> handler2
```

```
| ExceptionN -> handlerN
```

Multiple exceptions can be handled by specifying multiple pattern-matching clauses within the with block.

A practical example often seen in file I/O operations is handling the absence of a file. Consider the following code snippet:

```
exception FileNotFound of string

let read_file filename =
  if not (Sys.file_exists filename) then
    raise (FileNotFound "The specified file does not exist")
  else
    let ic = open_in filename in
    try
      let line = input_line ic in
      close_in ic;
      line
    with
    | End_of_file ->
      close_in_noerr ic;
      ""
    | exn ->
      close_in_noerr ic;
      raise exn
```

In this example:

- FileNotFound is raised if the specified file does not exist.
- The file is opened, and lines are read until an End_of_file exception is encountered.
- If any exception occurs (including End_of_file), the input channel ic is closed, ensuring no resource leaks occur.
- Any other exceptions are re-raised after closing the file, allowing external handlers to process them.

The exn pattern matches any exception, enabling a general handler for unforeseen cases, increasing the robustness of the error management.

In the context of complex systems, extensive error handling strategies may involve custom logging, aggregating exceptions, or error-flow tracing. Here is an extended example that demonstrates using the Result type to encapsulate exceptions in computations, facilitating a functional error-handling approach:

```
let capture_exception f x =
  try
    Ok (f x)
```

```
  with
  | MyException msg -> Error msg

let process_data x =
  match capture_exception risk_function x with
  | Ok result -> print_endline ("Success: " ^ string_of_int result)
  | Error msg -> print_endline ("Error: " ^ msg)
```

In this code, the capture_exception function wraps a computation, converting exceptions into Result types, either returning Ok with the result or Error with the exception message. The process_data function demonstrates how to use this mechanism to handle errors functionally.

Understanding and implementing efficient exception handling mechanisms are essential for creating robust OCaml applications, enabling developers to manage and mitigate the impact of runtime anomalies efficiently.

3.5 Option and Result Types

In OCaml, handling absence of a value or errors in a type-safe manner is essential for writing robust code. The option and result types provide powerful tools to achieve this. These types help in communicating the possibility of absence of values or errors explicitly and handling them gracefully.

The option type is used when a value might be present or absent. It is defined as follows:

```
type 'a option = None | Some of 'a
```

Here, option is a polymorphic variant type, meaning it can be used with any data type. The None variant indicates the absence of a value, and the Some variant contains a value of type 'a. Consider the following example demonstrating the use of the option type:

```
let divide x y =
  if y = 0 then None
  else Some (x / y)
```

In this example, the divide function returns an int option. If the division is by zero, it returns None; otherwise, it returns Some quotient. Usage of this function can be illustrated as follows:

```
match divide 10 2 with
| None -> Printf.printf "Cannot divide by zero\n"
| Some quotient -> Printf.printf "Quotient: %d\n" quotient
```

```
match divide 10 0 with
| None -> Printf.printf "Cannot divide by zero\n"
| Some quotient -> Printf.printf "Quotient: %d\n" quotient
```

The pattern matching ensures that both cases (None and Some) are handled explicitly, promoting safer and more predictable code.

The result type is particularly useful for functions that may fail and need to provide an error message or value. It is defined as follows:

```
type ('a, 'b) result = Ok of 'a | Error of 'b
```

The result type is also polymorphic, but it has two type parameters: one for the success case ('a) and one for the error case ('b). This allows for more expressive error handling. Here is an example function that uses the result type:

```
let safeDivide x y =
  if y = 0 then Error "Division by zero"
  else Ok (x / y)
```

The safeDivide function now returns an (int, string) result, where Ok int indicates a successful division and Error string carries an error message. A typical use of this function would look like this:

```
match safeDivide 10 2 with
| Error msg -> Printf.printf "Error: %s\n" msg
| Ok quotient -> Printf.printf "Quotient: %d\n" quotient

match safeDivide 10 0 with
| Error msg -> Printf.printf "Error: %s\n" msg
| Ok quotient -> Printf.printf "Quotient: %d\n" quotient
```

Both the option and result types enhance the readability and safety of OCaml code by explicitly encoding the possibility of absence and error, making it harder for bugs related to invalid assumptions about the presence of values or successful computations to slip through.

For convenience and to avoid repetitive pattern matching, OCaml provides several utility functions. For the option type, functions such as option and default are frequently used. Here is a demonstration using these utilities:

```
let optionDefault default = function
  | None -> default
  | Some x -> x

let value = optionDefault 0 (Some 10) (* returns 10 *)
let value = optionDefault 0 None (* returns 0 *)
```

For the result type, utility functions like Result.get_ok and Result.get_-

error are used:

```
let resultOk = Ok 10
let resultError = Error "Something went wrong"

let okValue = Result.get_ok resultOk (* returns 10 *)
let errorMsg = Result.get_error resultError (* returns "Something went wrong" *)
```

Handle cases where values might be absent or errors might occur by incorporating option and result types into your OCaml programs. They are central concepts for writing maintainable and reliable software in OCaml.

3.6 Recursive Functions

Recursive functions are fundamental to functional programming and are particularly powerful in OCaml. They provide a mechanism to solve problems by breaking them down into smaller, more manageable subproblems of the same nature. A function is recursive if it calls itself within its definition. Recursive functions can be either direct or mutually recursive.

Direct Recursion: In direct recursion, a function directly calls itself. Consider the classic example of computing the factorial of a number. The factorial of a non-negative integer n (denoted as $n!$) is the product of all positive integers less than or equal to n. It is defined recursively as:

$$\begin{cases} 0! = 1 & \text{(Base Case)} \\ n! = n \times (n-1)! & \text{(Recursive Case)} \end{cases}$$

The following OCaml code demonstrates a direct recursive implementation of the factorial function:

```
let rec factorial n =
  if n = 0 then 1
  else n * factorial (n - 1)
```

In this implementation, the function factorial is defined with the keyword rec, which is mandatory for self-referential functions. The base case checks if $n = 0$. If true, it returns 1. Otherwise, it computes $n \times \text{factorial}(n-1)$, thereby calling itself with $n-1$.

Mutual Recursion: In mutual recursion, two or more functions call each other. For instance, consider the following example involving two mutually recursive functions is_even and is_odd:

```
let rec is_even n =
  if n = 0 then true
  else is_odd (n - 1)

and is_odd n =
  if n = 0 then false
  else is_even (n - 1)
```

Here, is_even checks if a number is even by a base case of $n = 0$ and returns true. If not, it calls is_odd with $n - 1$. Similarly, is_odd returns false for $n = 0$ and calls is_even otherwise. The mutual references between these functions necessitate the use of the and keyword.

Tail Recursion: In functional programming, tail recursion is an important optimization technique where the recursive call is the last operation performed by the function. This allows the compiler to optimize the recursive call to prevent excessive stack growth, effectively converting the recursion into iteration.

Consider a tail-recursive version of the factorial function:

```
let factorial n =
  let rec aux n acc =
    if n = 0 then acc
    else aux (n - 1) (n * acc)
  in aux n 1
```

Here, aux is an auxiliary function that carries an acc (accumulator) parameter to store intermediate results. The recursive call to aux is the last operation in the function, thereby making it tail-recursive.

Recursive Data Structures: Recursive functions are often used with recursive data structures such as lists. For example, consider the function to compute the length of a list:

```
let rec length = function
  | [] -> 0
  | _::t -> 1 + length t
```

In this code, length uses pattern matching to check if the list is empty ([]). If empty, it returns 0. Otherwise, it decomposes the list into its head and tail, and recursively computes the length of the tail.

Practical Example: Consider a function to compute the greatest common divisor (GCD) of two integers using the Euclidean algorithm:

```
let rec gcd a b =
  if b = 0 then a
  else gcd b (a mod b)
```

This function recursively calls itself with the parameters b and $a \mod b$, until b becomes 0. The recursion terminates when $b = 0$, and the function returns a as the GCD.

Recursive functions, when used judiciously, provide elegant solutions to complex problems and allow for clear and concise code. However, understanding the base and recursive cases, as well as ensuring tail recursion when appropriate, is essential for writing efficient recursive functions in OCaml.

3.7 Higher-Order Functions

Higher-order functions play a critical role in OCaml programming by enabling functions to take other functions as arguments or return them as results. This feature augments the flexibility and expressiveness of the language, allowing for more abstract and concise code structures. Understanding how to construct and utilize higher-order functions is indispensable for mastering OCaml.

A higher-order function can be expressed in its simplest form by defining a function that takes another function as a parameter. Let's consider a basic example of a higher-order function:

```
let apply_twice f x = f (f x)


In this definition, \texttt{apply\_twice} is a function that accepts two parameters: a
     function \texttt{f} and a value \texttt{x}. The body of \texttt{apply\_twice}
     applies the function \texttt{f} twice to \texttt{x}.

Consider using \texttt{apply\_twice} with a simple arithmetic function like adding
     one:

\begin{lstlisting}
let add_one x = x + 1
let result = apply_twice add_one 5
```

The resulting value of result will be:

```
7
```

This result is derived by first applying add_one to 5, producing 6, and then applying add_one again to 6, yielding 7.

Higher-order functions can also be used to create more complex operations, such as function composition. Function composition involves combining two or more functions to form a new function. Here's an example of how you can define a composition function:

```
let compose f g x = f (g x)
```

The compose function takes two functions f and g, and returns a new function that applies g to its argument, then applies f to the result. For example:

```
let square x = x * x
let increment_and_square = compose square add_one
let result = increment_and_square 3
```

The value of result will be:

```
16
```

Firstly, add_one is applied to 3, resulting in 4, and then square is applied to 4, resulting in 16.

In addition to these simple examples, higher-order functions are fundamental to several powerful OCaml abstractions. For instance, map and fold functions are quintessential higher-order functions extensively used with lists or other data structures. The List.map function applies a given function to each element of a list:

```
let double x = x * 2
let doubled_list = List.map double [1; 2; 3; 4]
```

After execution, doubled_list will hold the values:

```
[2; 4; 6; 8]
```

Another central higher-order function is the List.fold_left function, which accumulates values from a list using a specified binary function. An example of summing a list of integers with List.fold_left:

```
let sum = List.fold_left ( + ) 0 [1; 2; 3; 4; 5]
```

The value of sum will be:

```
15
```

Patterns of higher-order functions also extend to scenarios where functions need to return other functions. This is useful in creating currified forms of multi-argument functions. In OCaml, functions by default are curried, but you can explicitly define functions that return functions:

```
let add x y = x + y
let add_five = add 5
let result = add_five 10
```

The value of result will be:

15

The add function is a two-argument function, but by providing the first argument 5, we obtain another function add_five which only requires one argument. This property is particularly useful in partial application and point-free style of function definitions.

OCaml also supports anonymous functions (lambdas) that are frequently employed with higher-order functions. An example using an anonymous function with List.map:

```
let squared_list = List.map (fun x -> x * x) [1; 2; 3; 4]
```

The value of squared_list will be:

```
[1; 4; 9; 16]
```

The use of anonymous functions facilitates inline definitions without the need to create separately named functions, thereby providing an elegant and modular approach. As functions in OCaml are first-class values, they can be assigned to variables, passed as arguments, and returned from other functions, thereby promoting a functional programming paradigm.

Mastering higher-order functions involves recognizing and leveraging these patterns to write more abstract, modular, and reusable code.

3.8 Combining Control Structures

In OCaml programming, control structures form the backbone of logical decision-making and flow control. Mastering individual elements like conditional statements, loops, and pattern matching is quintessential; however, the real strength of a seasoned programmer lies in the ability to combine these constructs effectively. This section examines various ways to intertwine OCaml's control structures for crafting robust, efficient, and readable code.

Conditional Statements and Pattern Matching

Combining conditional statements with pattern matching enhances the precision of your checks and the conciseness of your code. Consider a scenario where we need to handle input differently based on certain conditions and patterns:

```
let process_input input =
  match input with
  | [] -> "Empty list"
```

```
  | [x] when x > 0 -> "Single positive element"
  | [x] when x <= 0 -> "Single non-positive element"
  | x::xs when x mod 2 = 0 -> "Starts with an even number"
  | x::xs -> "Starts with an odd number"
```

In this example, the pattern matching is augmented with when clauses, enabling additional conditional checks on the matched patterns. This blending of conditions and patterns can simplify the code and make it more expressive compared to multiple nested if-then-else statements.

Pattern Matching and Loops

OCaml's pattern matching can be used inside loops to manage complex data structures more intuitively. Let's examine a function that processes elements of a list differently based on their patterns:

```
let rec process_list = function
  | [] -> ()
  | h::t ->
    (match h with
      | 0 -> Printf.printf "Zero found\n"
      | x when x > 0 -> Printf.printf "Positive number: %d\n" x
      | _ -> Printf.printf "Negative number: %d\n" h);
    process_list t

let () = process_list [3; -1; 0; 5; -2]
```

This recursive function demonstrates pattern matching within a loop, where the match statement is used to differentiate between Zero, positive, and negative numbers. The integration of these constructs allows for a clean and comprehensive traversal of the list.

Exception Handling in Loops and Pattern Matching

Exception handling is crucial for managing unexpected conditions and errors. By combining exception handling with loops and pattern matching, we can ensure graceful handling of potential faults:

```
exception NegativeNumber of int

let rec safe_process_list = function
  | [] -> ()
  | h::t ->
    (try
       match h with
       | 0 -> Printf.printf "Zero found\n"
       | x when x > 0 -> Printf.printf "Positive number: %d\n" x
       | x -> raise (NegativeNumber x)
     with
     | NegativeNumber x -> Printf.printf "Exception: Negative number %d handled\n"
         x);
    safe_process_list t

let () = safe_process_list [3; -1; 0; 5; -2]
```

In the above function, an exception is raised and caught within the pattern matching construct inside a loop. This approach ensures that each element is processed, and exceptions are handled locally without disrupting the overall program flow.

Higher-Order Functions and Control Structures

Higher-order functions, such as List.map and List.filter, often pair effectively with OCaml's control structures. By passing in functions that incorporate conditional statements or pattern matching, you can write more abstract and reusable code:

```
let is_even x = x mod 2 = 0
let double_if_even lst =
  List.map (fun x -> if is_even x then x * 2 else x) lst

let () =
  let result = double_if_even [1; 2; 3; 4; 5] in
  List.iter (Printf.printf "%d ") result
```

Here, the function double_if_even uses List.map to apply a conditional doubling to each element. The combination of higher-order functions with if-then-else statements provides a powerful tool for list transformations and other operations.

Recursive Functions with Multiple Control Structures

Combining recursion with various control structures allows you to solve complex problems elegantly. Consider a function that traverses a tree, applying different operations based on node properties:

```
type 'a tree =
  | Empty
  | Node of 'a * 'a tree * 'a tree

let rec sum_tree = function
  | Empty -> 0
  | Node (value, left, right) ->
    let left_sum = sum_tree left in
    let right_sum = sum_tree right in
    value + left_sum + right_sum

let t = Node (5, Node (3, Empty, Empty), Node (8, Empty, Node (6, Empty, Empty)))

let () = Printf.printf "Sum of tree: %d\n" (sum_tree t)
```

In this example, the sum_tree function recursively sums the values of all nodes in a binary tree. The combination of recursive functions with conditional checks (match constructs) enables clear and concise tree traversal and aggregation.

The examples provided herein illustrate that combining control structures in OCaml enhances code expressiveness, efficiency, and robustness. Through strategic use of conditional statements, loops, pattern matching, exception handling, and higher-order functions, programmers can develop more sophisticated and maintainable solutions.

Chapter 4

Functional Programming

This chapter introduces the core concepts of functional programming in OCaml, focusing on immutability and the avoidance of side effects. We will explore the significance of first-class and anonymous functions, closures, and function composition. The concepts of partial application and currying will be discussed, and the chapter will revisit higher-order functions and common functional programming patterns and paradigms, providing a comprehensive understanding of functional programming principles in OCaml.

4.1 Introduction to Functional Programming

Functional programming is a programming paradigm where programs are constructed by applying and composing functions. In OCaml, functional programming forms the backbone of the language's design. It emphasizes immutability, first-class functions, and the avoidance of side effects.

The foundational principle of functional programming is that computation should be treated as the evaluation of mathematical functions. Unlike imperative programming, which changes state and relies on the concept of an execution sequence, functional programming utilizes expressions rather than statements.

Consider the simple arithmetic expression:

```
let result = (3 + 4) * 2;;
```

In this example, the computation $(3 + 4)$ results in 7, and the multiplication by 2 produces the final result 14. The computation is expressed in terms of evaluating expressions rather than executing a series of steps.

An essential concept in functional programming is the treatment of functions themselves as first-class citizens in the language. This means functions can be assigned to variables, passed as arguments, and returned from other functions. Consider the following example in OCaml:

```
let add x y = x + y;;
```

Here, add is a function that takes two arguments, x and y, and returns their sum. Once defined, add can be used like any other value:

```
let sum = add 3 4;;
```

This assigns the value 7 to the variable sum.

Moreover, functions can be defined anonymously using lambda expressions. Anonymous functions are useful when a function is needed only for a short period. Instead of giving the function a name, a lambda expression creates a function and returns it as a value. In OCaml, a lambda expression is written using the fun keyword. Consider the following example:

```
let increment = fun x -> x + 1;;
```

Here, increment is a function that takes an argument x and returns x incremented by one. This lambda expression can be used in various contexts, such as higher-order functions.

Speaking of higher-order functions, these are functions that take other functions as arguments or return functions as results. They are a defining characteristic of functional programming and are widely used for tasks such as function composition, mapping, and reducing lists. For example, the List.map function in OCaml applies a function to each element of a list:

```
let double x = x * 2;;
let doubled_list = List.map double [1; 2; 3; 4];;
```

In this example, List.map applies the double function to each element of the list [1; 2; 3; 4], producing the list [2; 4; 6; 8].

Immutability is another cornerstone of functional programming. In an immutable paradigm, data does not change state or value once created. This attribute prevents side effects, leading to more predictable and robust code. Instead of modifying an existing value, functions in a functional program produce new values. Consider the following example:

```
let x = 10;;
let y = x + 5;;
```

Once x is bound to 10, its value remains unchanged throughout its scope. The expression x + 5 results in 15, which is assigned to y. The original value of x is not modified.

Functional programming in OCaml also supports powerful abstractions such as pattern matching, which enables concise and clear program expressions. Pattern matching allows the program to deconstruct data structures and bind variables to values based on the shape and content of the data. For example, consider the following code to handle a list:

```
let rec sum_list lst =
  match lst with
  | [] -> 0
  | head :: tail -> head + sum_list tail;;
```

In this recursive function sum_list, pattern matching determines if the list lst is empty or if it has a head element and a tail (another list). The function returns 0 for an empty list, and for a non-empty list, it adds the head to the result of summing the tail. This elegant way of handling various data forms without complex control structures is a key feature of functional programming.

It is crucial to grasp the foundational principles that drive functional programming in OCaml. Understanding first-class functions, anonymous functions, higher-order functions, immutability, and pattern matching will provide a robust basis for progressing through more advanced concepts and paradigms in functional programming.

4.2 Immutability and Side Effects

Immutability and the avoidance of side effects constitute the foundation of functional programming in OCaml. Understanding these concepts is essential for writing robust and predictable code.

In functional programming, **immutability** refers to the idea that once a value is created, it cannot be changed. This is in contrast to imperative programming paradigms, where variables can be assigned new values during their lifecycle. Immutability enhances predictability, simplifies debugging, and makes concurrent programming more manageable by eliminating race conditions.

For example, in an imperative language, you might have:

```
let x = 10;;
x = x + 1;; (* Increment x, imperatively *)
```

In contrast, with OCaml's immutable variables, you would instead create a new value:

```
let x = 10;;
let x' = x + 1;; (* Create a new value x' *)
```

The variable x remains unchanged, and any subsequent operations use x' instead. This distinction prevents unintended modifications and ensures consistent state.

Side effects in programming refer to any change in state or observable interaction with the outside world that occurs during the execution of a function. Functional programming principles aim to avoid side effects. Functions that avoid side effects are called *pure functions*.

A function is pure if:

- Its output value is the same for the same input values.
- It does not produce any observable side effects.

Consider the following OCaml function:

```
let add a b = a + b;;
```

The function add is pure because it always returns the same result given the same arguments and does not affect any state outside its scope.

In contrast, the following function has a side effect:

```
let print_and_add a b =
  let result = a + b in
  print_int result;
  result;;
```

Here, print_and_add not only returns the sum of a and b, but it also prints the result to the console. The act of printing is a side effect because it affects the outside world.

Pure functions are advantageous because they are easier to reason about. Their behavior is predictable as they do not rely on or change any external state. This makes them more testable; given the same inputs, they always produce the same outputs.

Another advantage of immutability and purity is that it facilitates expression verification. Suppose you have a series of expressions where each depends on the previous one. With immutability and no side effects, these expressions remain consistent throughout the scope they are defined, eliminating unexpected changes in intermediate calculations.

Additionally, when writing concurrent or parallel programs, immutable data structures prevent issues related to concurrent modifications. Immutable data structures do not require locks or other synchronization mechanisms, reducing overhead and complexity.

Consider the following scenario involving concurrency:

```
let shared_resource = ref 0;;
```

Using imperative style, concurrent threads might increment shared_resource leading to race conditions. Functions relying on side effects thus require careful handling to ensure thread safety. Immutability mitigates these issues naturally:

```
let increment x = x + 1;;
let results = List.map increment [1; 2; 3; 4; 5];;
```

increment is a pure function without side effects. Mapping it over a list of values [1; 2; 3; 4; 5] ensures that each operation is independent of the others, making it intrinsically thread-safe.

One should note that OCaml supports working with mutable states when necessary, using references and mutable data types. However, it is prudent to default to immutability and favor it wherever possible. The mutable state is managed using ref and mutable record fields, though this should be done cautiously to avoid reintroducing the problems functional programming aims to circumvent.

To summarize, adhering to immutability and avoiding side effects are crucial practices in functional programming with OCaml. These principles foster predictable, maintainable, and concurrent-safe code, thus enhancing the overall robustness and reliability of programs written in OCaml. These principles, combined with other functional programming constructs, form the cornerstone of proficient OCaml programming.

4.3 First-Class Functions

In functional programming, functions are first-class citizens. This concept entails that functions in OCaml can be passed as arguments to other functions, returned as values from other functions, and assigned to variables. First-class functions allow for a higher level of abstraction in programming, and they are a cornerstone for many advanced functional programming techniques.

To illustrate the significance of first-class functions, consider the following basic example where we define a function and assign it to a variable:

```
let add x y = x + y
let add_function = add
```

Here, add is a simple function that returns the sum of its two arguments. The function add is assigned to the variable add_function. We can now use add_function as if it were the original add function:

```
let result = add_function 2 3
```

result = 5

In this example, the variable result is assigned the value 5, which is the result of calling add_function with the arguments 2 and 3.

Next, let us delve deeper into passing functions as arguments to other functions. This feature is extensively leveraged in higher-order functions. Consider a function that takes another function and a list as its arguments, applying the function to each element of the list:

```
let apply_function f lst = List.map f lst
```

Here, apply_function is a higher-order function that takes a function f and a list lst. It uses the List.map function to apply f to each element of lst. An example usage is as follows:

```
let square x = x * x
let numbers = [1; 2; 3; 4; 5]
let squares = apply_function square numbers
```

squares = [1; 4; 9; 16; 25]

In this case, square is applied to each element of the list numbers, resulting in the list squares containing the squares of the original numbers.

A more complex and useful feature derived from first-class functions is the ability to return functions from other functions. This capability forms the foundation for creating advanced higher-order functions and implementing function currying. Let us consider an example where a function generates another function:

```
let create_adder x =
  let adder y = x + y in
  adder
```

In this example, create_adder is a function that returns another function adder. The returned function adder adds its argument y to the argument x of create_adder. This can be utilized as follows:

```
let add_five = create_adder 5
let result = add_five 10
```

result = 15

add_five becomes a new function that adds 5 to its input argument. When add_five 10 is called, the result is 15.

Furthermore, first-class functions enable the concise expression of complex operations. Function composition is one such operation where two or more functions are combined to form a new function. Consider the following example:

```
let compose f g x = f (g x)
```

The compose function takes two functions f and g, and returns a new function that applies g to its input and then f to the result. Usage is illustrated below:

```
let double x = x * 2
let increment x = x + 1
let double_then_increment = compose increment double
let result = double_then_increment 3
```

result = 7

In this scenario, double_then_increment composed of double and increment functions is applied to 3. First, 3 is doubled to 6, then 1 is added to yield 7.

First-class functions also facilitate the creation of generic and reusable code by allowing the encapsulation of behavior within functions that can be dynamically manipulated and invoked. These advanced capabilities often lead to the development of elegant, concise, and powerful programs.

The concept of first-class functions is not just a theoretical construct but a practical tool that significantly impacts the design and implementation of software. Understanding and utilizing first-class functions effectively is essential for mastering OCaml and exploiting its functional programming paradigm to its full potential.

4.4 Anonymous Functions

Anonymous functions in OCaml are functions that are defined without being bound to a specific name. These functions allow more concise code, particularly useful when the function is used only in a limited scope. Anonymous functions are also referred to as *lambda functions* or *lambda expressions*. Their syntax in OCaml employs the fun keyword.

The general syntax of an anonymous function in OCaml is as follows:

```
fun parameter1 parameter2 ... parameterN -> expression
```

Here, parameter1, parameter2, up to parameterN are the parameters passed to the function, and expression denotes the function's body.

Consider the following basic example to illustrate an anonymous function that adds two numbers:

```
let sum = fun x y -> x + y
```

This anonymous function takes two parameters, x and y, and returns their sum. The function itself is bound to the variable sum.
Evaluating sum 5 7 would produce the output:

```
12
```

Anonymous functions are particularly powerful when passed as arguments to higher-order functions. For instance, the List.map function applies a given function to each element of a list. Using an anonymous function, we can succinctly express our intentions:

```
let incremented_list = List.map (fun x -> x + 1) [1; 2; 3; 4; 5]
```

This code creates a new list, each element of which is the result of incrementing the respective element of the input list by 1. The result of incremented_list would be:

```
[2; 3; 4; 5; 6]
```

When defining anonymous functions with multiple parameters, the syntax remains straightforward. Consider a function that performs element-wise addition of two lists. Using the List.map2 function combined with an anonymous function allows for a clear and concise expression:

```
let list_sum = List.map2 (fun x y -> x + y) [1; 2; 3] [4; 5; 6]
```

Here, List.map2 applies the anonymous function fun x y -> x + y to each corresponding pair of elements from the two input lists. The resulting list would be:

```
[5; 7; 9]
```

Anonymous functions can also be nested within other functions. This is useful when the function's use is confined to the scope of another function and does not warrant a separate named definition. Consider an example involving filtering and mapping over a list to produce a list of squares of even numbers:

```
let squares_of_evens lst =
  lst
  |> List.filter (fun x -> x mod 2 = 0)
  |> List.map (fun x -> x * x)
```

In this code, List.filter uses an anonymous function fun x -> x mod 2 = 0 to select only the even numbers, and List.map subsequently applies another anonymous function fun x -> x * x to square each of the filtered numbers. Given an input list [1; 2; 3; 4; 5; 6], the function squares_of_evens would produce:

```
[4; 16; 36]
```

Anonymous functions also support partial application, enabling the creation of new functions by fixing some arguments of an existing function. Consider the following example:

```
let add = fun x y -> x + y
let add_five = add 5
```

In this code, add is an anonymous function that adds two numbers. By partially applying it with 5, we create add_five, a new function that adds 5 to its argument. Thus, add_five 10 would produce:

```
15
```

Anonymous functions are essential tools in functional programming, enabling succinct and expressive coding patterns. They can encapsulate behaviors dynamically and often eliminate the need for extraneous named functions.

4.5 Closures

In functional programming, particularly in OCaml, a **closure** is a first-class function with free variables that are bound in the lexical scope. The concept of closures is integral to functional programming as it enables functions to carry an environment with them, effectively capturing the variables from their creation context.

To fully understand closures, we need to grasp the idea of lexical scoping and how functions can "capture" variables. Let us examine the following OCaml code snippet:

```
let create_multiplier factor =
  let multiply_by_factor x = x * factor in
  multiply_by_factor
```

Here, create_multiplier is a function that takes a parameter factor and returns another function multiply_by_factor. The returned function, multiply_by_factor, uses the factor that was present in the environment when multiply_by_factor was defined. The factor variable is the free variable captured by the closure.

To utilize this code, we can write:

```
let times_two = create_multiplier 2
let result = times_two 5
```

In this example, times_two is a closure. When we call times_two 5, the function multiply_by_factor is executed with x = 5 and uses the factor = 2 captured when times_two was created, yielding the result 10.

The ability to capture variables results in powerful and flexible code. It allows for encapsulation of the state within functions without using objects or mutable data. The following code illustrates how closures can maintain state:

```
let counter () =
  let count = ref 0 in
  let increment () =
    count := !count + 1;
    !count
  in
  increment
```

Here, counter returns a closure increment that maintains a reference to count. Each call to increment modifies and returns the updated value of count. Use it as follows:

```
let c = counter ()
let _ = print_int (c ()) (* Output: 1 *)
let _ = print_int (c ()) (* Output: 2 *)
let _ = print_int (c ()) (* Output: 3 *)
```

Notice how count is retained across multiple calls to c. This aspect of closures underpins many functional programming techniques, enabling function composition, memoization, and event handling.

Closures also encourage the creation of higher-order functions. Higher-order functions are functions that take other functions as parameters or return them. They form the backbone of functional programming by facilitating operations like map, filter, and reduce. Consider this higher-order function:

```
let apply_twice f x =
  f (f x)
```

apply_twice is a higher-order function that takes another function f and a value x, applying f to x twice. Using closures, it can seamlessly capture and reuse the given function without any loss of context.

Moreover, closures support partial application, where a function is applied to arguments one at a time, returning a new function that takes the remaining arguments. This can significantly simplify code, enhancing readability and maintainability. Consider this example:

```
let add a b = a + b
let increment = add 1
let result = increment 4 (* Output: 5 *)
```

Here, increment is a partially-applied function and, consequently, a closure. When increment is called with 4, it uses the captured value 1 from its environment and outputs 5.

In functional programming, the utilization of closures is pivotal. They provide a means for defining functions with preserved state and lexically-scoped variables, empowering developers to write modular and composable code. This section has demonstrated how closures work, their significance in maintaining encapsulated environments, and how they facilitate functional programming paradigms in OCaml.

4.6 Function Composition

Function composition is a central concept in functional programming, allowing for the combination of multiple functions to produce a new function. By composing functions, complex operations can be built from simpler ones in a concise and readable manner. This section examines how to compose functions in OCaml, leveraging the language's capabilities to succinctly express function composition.

In OCaml, function composition can be achieved using the composition operator (%>). This operator takes two functions as arguments and returns a new function that represents the composition of the two. For instance, given two functions f and g, the composition f %> g applies f to an argument and then applies g to the result.

To define the composition operator (%>), we can use the following code snippet:

```
let ( %> ) f g x = g (f x)
```

In this definition, f and g are functions, and x is the argument to be passed through the composed function. The composition operator (%>) can now be used to combine functions as shown in the following example:

```
let square x = x * x
let increment x = x + 1

let increment_then_square = increment %> square

let result = increment_then_square 3
```

The expected output of the above code when invoking increment_then_square 3 is:

```
16
```

Here, increment_then_square is a composed function that first increments its argument by 1 and then squares the result. Specifically, increment_then_square 3 computes increment 3 to yield 4 and subsequently computes square 4 to yield 16.

Composition not only improves code readability but also encourages the construction of reusable and modular code. By abstracting complex transformations into small, composable functions, it becomes easier to reason about the program and verify its correctness.

Let's consider another example involving more complex transformations. Assume we need to normalize a list of floating-point numbers by applying a series of functions:

1. Compute the absolute value. 2. Scale the value by a fixed factor. 3. Clamp the value to a predefined range.

These transformations can be individually defined and then composed to achieve the desired result:

```
let abs_val x = abs_float x
let scale factor x = x *. factor
let clamp min max x = min (max x min) max

let normalize = abs_val %> scale 0.5 %> clamp 0.0 1.0

let values = [-1.0; 0.0; 0.5; 1.0; 2.0]

let normalized_values = List.map normalize values
```

The expected output of the execution is:

```
[0.5; 0.0; 0.25; 0.5; 1.0]
```

Here, the normalize function is composed of abs_val, scale 0.5, and clamp 0.0 1.0. This combined function computes the absolute value of each element, scales it by 0.5, and then clamps it to the range [0.0, 1.0]. The List.map function applies normalize to each element in the list values, yielding the list of normalized values.

Function composition empowers the development of flexible and reusable code components. Moreover, it aligns with the principles of immutability and side-effect-free computations, which are central to functional programming.

When composing functions, it is essential to account for the order of application. The operator (%>) applies functions right to left, meaning the function on the right is applied after the function on the left. In some cases, alternate composition orders might be needed, and this can be accomplished by nesting the applications manually or defining additional composition operators.

Another useful pattern is the pipeline operator (%>) which can be used to chain function applications smoothly:

```
let normalize_pipeline x =
  x
  %> abs_val
  %> scale 0.5
  %> clamp 0.0 1.0

let normalized_values_pipeline = List.map normalize_pipeline values
```

The expected output remains the same:

```
[0.5; 0.0; 0.25; 0.5; 1.0]
```

The pipeline operator enhances readability by denoting a clear sequence of function applications, similar to a series of transformations where each step is visually and sequentially evident. This pattern increases the clarity of data flow, promoting better comprehension and maintenance of the code.

By employing function composition, developers can construct intricate behaviors through the combination of simple functions, fostering code reuse, readability, and maintainability in OCaml programs.

4.7 Partial Application

Partial application is a fundamental concept in functional programming that enables the creation of new functions by pre-fixing some arguments of an existing function. This technique is particularly valuable in OCaml, where functions are curried by default. Currying transforms a function that takes multiple arguments into a sequence of function applications, each with a single argument. Consequently, we can leverage partial application to simplify function definitions and improve code modularity and reusability.

Consider the following function that adds three integers:

```
let add_three_numbers x y z = x + y + z
```

Here, add_three_numbers expects three arguments (x, y, z) and returns their sum. Using partial application, we can create a new function by fixing one or more arguments. For instance, to create a function that adds 10 to two other numbers:

```
let add_ten_to_two_numbers = add_three_numbers 10
```

In this example, add_ten_to_two_numbers is a new function that takes two arguments. When called, it adds 10 to the sum of these two arguments:

```
let result = add_ten_to_two_numbers 5 7
(* result = 10 + 5 + 7 = 22 *)
```

The principle of partial application aligns with the notion of higher-order functions, allowing us to return functions as first-class values. This approach can be particularly powerful when combined with higher-order functions such as map, filter, and fold. Consider the example where we want to create a function that multiplies an entire list of integers by 3.

First, define a multiplication function:

```
let multiply x y = x * y
```

Next, create a partially applied function that always multiplies by 3:

```
let multiply_by_3 = multiply 3
```

Finally, use List.map to apply multiply_by_3 to each element in a list:

```
let numbers = [1; 2; 3; 4; 5]
let multiplied_numbers = List.map multiply_by_3 numbers
(* multiplied_numbers = [3; 6; 9; 12; 15] *)
```

Another common use case of partial application is in combination with functions that take higher-order functions as arguments. Assume we have a function apply_twice that applies a given function twice to an argument:

```
let apply_twice f x = f (f x)
```

By partially applying a function, we can customize how apply_twice behaves. Here, we simply multiply an integer by 2 twice:

```
let double = multiply 2
let result = apply_twice double 5
(* result = double (double 5) = double 10 = 20 *)
```

Understanding partial application allows for more versatile and expressive function definitions. For example, it simplifies the invocation of functions in various scopes and contexts. Here's an illustration of how partial application can be utilized in a sorting algorithm:

```
let compare_lengths s1 s2 = compare (String.length s1) (String.length s2)
let sort_by_length = List.sort compare_lengths
let words = ["apple"; "banana"; "kiwi"; "grape"]
let sorted_words = sort_by_length words
(* sorted_words = ["kiwi"; "apple"; "grape"; "banana"] *)
```

The compare_lengths function compares the lengths of two strings, and the sort_by_length function sorts a list of strings based on their lengths. The sort_by_length function is defined using partial application, making the code clearer and more concise.

In more complex scenarios, partial application can also facilitate the creation of specialized utility functions from more generic ones. Suppose we have a logger function that logs messages with varying levels of importance:

```
type log_level = Info | Warning | Error

let log level msg =
  let level_str = match level with
    | Info -> "Info"
    | Warning -> "Warning"
    | Error -> "Error"
  in
  Printf.printf "[%s]: %s\n" level_str msg
```

Using partial application, we can create specific logger functions for each log level:

```
let log_info = log Info
let log_warning = log Warning
let log_error = log Error
```

These partially applied functions streamline logging at different levels:

```
log_info "This is an information message."
(* Output: [Info]: This is an information message. *)
log_warning "This is a warning message."
(* Output: [Warning]: This is a warning message. *)
log_error "This is an error message."
(* Output: [Error]: This is an error message. *)
```

Partial application thus embodies the principles of functional programming by promoting immutability, function reusability, and expressive code constructs, essential in mastering advanced OCaml programming.

4.8 Currying

Currying is a fundamental concept in functional programming that transforms a function with multiple arguments into a series of functions, each with a single argument. This technique allows for the partial application of functions, enabling greater modularity and reusability in code. Understanding currying in OCaml helps leverage its functional programming paradigm to write more concise and expressive programs.

In OCaml, a function that takes multiple arguments can be transformed into a sequence of functions, each taking a single argument. Consider the following example:

```
let add x y = x + y
```

The add function takes two arguments, x and y, and returns their sum. Using currying, add can be transformed into a series of functions:

```
let curry_add x = fun y -> x + y
```

Here, curry_add takes a single argument x and returns a new function that takes another argument y and returns the sum of x and y. The same effect is achieved using a more straightforward syntax in OCaml:

```
let curry_add x y = x + y
```

OCaml implicitly curries functions by default, so the above definition is equivalent to the manually curried function.

Currying enables partial application, where some arguments of a function are fixed, creating a new function that takes the remaining arguments. For example, using the curried version of add, we can create a new function that adds a specific value to its argument:

```
let add_five = curry_add 5
```

Here, add_five is a new function that adds 5 to its argument. Executing the function produces the following:

```
let result = add_five 10
```

The result will be 15, as add_five fixes the first argument of curry_add to 5 and then adds it to the second argument (10 in this case).

To further illustrate currying, consider a function that multiplies three numbers:

```
let multiply x y z = x * y * z
```

Using currying, multiply can be expressed as:

```
let curry_multiply x = fun y -> fun z -> x * y * z
```

In its curried form, curry_multiply takes an argument x, and returns a function that takes an argument y, which in turn returns a new function that takes an argument z and computes the product x * y * z. This chaining can be written more concisely in OCaml:

```
let curry_multiply x y z = x * y * z
```

Partial application with curried functions brings several benefits. For instance, we can create specialized versions of the multiplication function:

```
let double = curry_multiply 2
let triple = curry_multiply 3
```

Here, double is a function that takes two arguments and multiplies them by 2, and triple is a function that multiplies two arguments by 3. This approach demonstrates how currying can enhance code reusability and expressiveness.

Evaluation order in curried functions follows a left-to-right application. Each time a curried function is applied to an argument, a new function is returned that expects the following argument. This process continues until all arguments are supplied. For example:

```
let partial_multiply = curry_multiply 2 3
```

Here, partial_multiply is a function waiting for a single argument. Applying the remaining argument concludes the computation:

```
let final_result = partial_multiply 4
```

The final_result will be 24, as partial_multiply fixes the first two arguments to 2 and 3 respectively, and multiplies them with the third argument.

Lambda expressions can also be curried in a straightforward manner. Consider the following lambda expression for a function that adds three numbers:

```
let add_3_numbers = fun x -> fun y -> fun z -> x + y + z
```

This can be applied partially just like named curried functions:

```
let add_5_and_ = add_3_numbers 5
```

The add_5_and_ function now expects two more arguments to complete the sum, demonstrating how both named and anonymous functions (lambdas) benefit from currying and partial application.

To generalize, currying transforms an n-ary function into a chain of n functions, each with a single parameter. This transformation is valuable in functional programming for creating flexible, reusable code modules and for facilitating refined functional compositions.

Understanding currying is essential to mastering OCaml and functional programming principles. Currying simplifies function handling, enhances expressiveness, and enables partial application, which can be effectively used to improve code modularity and maintainability.

4.9 Higher-Order Functions Revisited

Higher-order functions are functions that take other functions as arguments or return functions as their output. In OCaml, higher-order functions are a cornerstone of functional programming, allowing for elegant and expressive code.

To recall, higher-order functions can be categorized into two types:

- *Functions that accept other functions as arguments*
- *Functions that return new functions as a result*

Let's delve deeper into these two categories with detailed examples and code snippets to reinforce understanding.

1. Functions that Accept Other Functions as Arguments.

Consider the map function, which applies a given function to each element of a list:

```
let rec map f lst =
  match lst with
  | [] -> []
  | x :: xs -> (f x) :: (map f xs)

(* Usage example *)
let increment x = x + 1
let numbers = [1; 2; 3; 4]
let incremented_numbers = map increment numbers
```

Here, map takes a function f and a list lst. It recursively applies f to each element of the list. The function increment is passed as an argument to map, incrementing each element of numbers.

2. Functions that Return New Functions as a Result.

Consider the compose function, which takes two functions f and g, and returns their composition:

```
let compose f g =
  fun x -> f (g x)

(* Usage example *)
let multiply_by_2 x = x * 2
let add_3 x = x + 3
let add_then_multiply = compose multiply_by_2 add_3
let result = add_then_multiply 5
```

In this case, compose takes two functions f and g, and returns a new function that, when called with an argument x, applies g to x and then f to the result of g x. This exemplifies creating higher-order functions that generate new functions based on input functions.

Both these properties enable complex operations to be abstracted into simple functional constructs, enhancing code readability and reusability.

Understanding higher-order functions provides the foundation to appreciate several advanced functional programming paradigms. Let's explore some pivotal applications, including their utility in common functional patterns.

a. Currying and Partial Application:

Higher-order functions play a crucial role in currying, a technique where a function is transformed into a sequence of functions, each with a single argument.

```
(* Non-curried version *)
let add (x, y) = x + y

(* Curried version *)
let add_curry x y = x + y

(* Partial application *)
let add_ten = add_curry 10
let result = add_ten 5
```

Here, add_curry is a curried version of the add function. Partial application allows us to fix some arguments of the function before utilization, showcasing flexibility in function invocation.

b. Functional Patterns and Paradigms:

Common patterns like fold, filter, and reduce extensively use higher-order functions.

Example of fold:

```
let rec fold_left f acc lst =
  match lst with
  | [] -> acc
  | x :: xs -> fold_left f (f acc x) xs

(* Usage example *)
let sum lst = fold_left (fun acc x -> acc + x) 0 lst
let numbers = [1; 2; 3; 4]
let sum_of_numbers = sum numbers
```

The function fold_left applies a binary function f cumulatively to the elements of list lst from left to right, using an initial accumulator acc. In this example, sum computes the sum of a list of numbers.

By revisiting higher-order functions and exemplifying their applications, we solidify the understanding that they are not mere abstract constructs but essential tools that provide powerful ways to write concise and expressive code.

4.10 Functional Patterns and Paradigms

In functional programming, specific patterns and paradigms guide the development of software by emphasizing functions and their applications. Understanding these patterns can significantly improve the quality and robustness of OCaml code.

Tail Recursion

Tail recursion is a form of recursion where the recursive call is the last operation in the function. This allows the compiler to optimize the recursive calls to iterative loops, preventing stack overflow errors in deep recursion cases. Consider the following example of a factorial function implemented using tail recursion:

```
let rec factorial_tail n acc =
  if n <= 1 then acc
  else factorial_tail (n - 1) (n * acc)
;;
```

Calling factorial_tail 5 1 will result in the computation of 5! efficiently without incurring deep stack usage. Here, acc accumulates the result progressively, and the function call itself is the final operation.

Map-Reduce Pattern

The map-reduce pattern involves applying a function to a list (or other collection) and then combining the results using a reducing function. This pattern is effective in parallel computing and data processing. In OCaml, List.map and List.fold_left embody this pattern. For example:

```
let square x = x * x;;

let squares = List.map square [1; 2; 3; 4; 5];;

let sum_of_squares = List.fold_left (+) 0 squares;;
```

Execution output:

```
squares: [1; 4; 9; 16; 25]
sum_of_squares: 55
```

Here, List.map applies the square function to each element of the list, and List.fold_left sums the squared values.

Pipelines and Composability

The pipeline operator |> passes the result of an expression as the input to the next function, promoting readability and composability. Consider transforming and filtering a list of integers:

```
let is_even x = x mod 2 = 0;;

let process_list lst =
  lst
  |> List.map square
  |> List.filter is_even
;;
```

Execution of process_list [1; 2; 3; 4; 5] will first square each value, then filter out the odd numbers. This use of the pipeline operator leads to clear, modular code construction.

Lazy Evaluation

OCaml supports lazy evaluation through the Lazy module. Lazy evaluation defers the computation of expressions until their values are needed, which can optimize performance and manage infinite data structures. An example would be:

```
let lazy_square x = lazy (x * x);;

let lazy_val = lazy_square 3;;

let force_val = Lazy.force lazy_val;;
```

Lazy.force evaluates the expression stored in the lazy value. Until then, the computation of $3 * 3$ is deferred.

Immutable Data Structures

Functional programming emphasizes immutability, where data structures are not altered once created. This leads to predictable and side-effect-free code. OCaml provides several immutable data structures, such as lists and tuples. For instance:

```
let my_list = [1; 2; 3];;

let new_list = 0 :: my_list;;
```

Here, my_list remains unmodified; new_list is a new list with 0 prepended.

Pattern Matching

Pattern matching in OCaml simplifies the deconstruction of data types and makes code more readable. It is particularly useful when working with variant types. An example:

```
type shape =
  | Circle of float
  | Rectangle of float * float
;;

let area s =
  match s with
  | Circle r -> 3.1415 *. r *. r
  | Rectangle (l, w) -> l *. w
;;
```

This function calculates the area of different shapes using pattern matching on the shape type.

Higher-Order Functions

Higher-order functions take other functions as arguments or return them as results. They are central to functional programming. Functions like map, filter, and fold are examples. Custom higher-order functions can also be created:

```
let apply_twice f x = f (f x);;

let double x = x * 2;;

let result = apply_twice double 3;;
```

Execution output:

```
result: 12
```

apply_twice applies the function f twice to the argument x.

Monad Pattern

Monads in OCaml manage side effects and represent computations as sequences of steps. They encapsulate behaviors like optionality, state, and I/O. Consider the option monad for handling computations that might fail:

```
let bind opt f =
  match opt with
  | Some x -> f x
  | None -> None
```

```
;;

let (>>=) = bind;;

let add_option opt1 opt2 =
  opt1 >>= fun x ->
  opt2 >>= fun y ->
  Some (x + y)
;;
```

Using Some 2 »= add_one »= add_one results in Some 4, chaining computations that may return None.

Embracing these paradigms cultivates an efficient, reliable, and expressive programming style, enhancing both the development experience and the resulting software quality. Understanding and applying these patterns enrich your OCaml programming toolbox, enabling the creation of elegant and maintainable code.

Chapter 5

Data Structures in OCaml

This chapter covers various data structures in OCaml, starting with lists and arrays and extending to records, variants, and tagged unions. We will explore the use and manipulation of dictionaries, hash tables, sets, and maps. Custom data types, tree and graph data structures will also be discussed, with a focus on their efficient utilization. The chapter aims to equip readers with a solid understanding of how to leverage OCaml's data structures for optimal performance in different programming scenarios.

5.1 Lists and Pattern Matching Revisited

Lists in OCaml are fundamental and versatile data structures. They allow for grouping of elements of the same type and offer numerous functions for manipulation. Lists are immutable, meaning that once they are created, their elements cannot be changed. This immutability is a key feature that underpins the reliability and predictability of functional programming. Pattern matching, another powerful feature of OCaml, enables the deconstruction of lists in a concise and readable manner.

The syntax for lists in OCaml is straightforward. Lists are written as elements separated by semicolons and enclosed in square brackets:

```
let lst = [1; 2; 3; 4; 5]
```

Empty lists are simply represented as:

```
let empty_list = []
```

A list can contain elements of any type, but once the type is set, all elements in the list must be of that type. For instance, a list of strings would look like:

```
let string_list = ["OCaml"; "Programming"; "Language"]
```

Pattern matching is a technique used to destructure and analyze the content of lists, enabling more straightforward and expressive code. The match statement is central to this technique. A simple pattern-matching example deconstructing a list is shown below:

```
let rec sum_list lst =
  match lst with
  | [] -> 0
  | head :: tail -> head + sum_list tail
```

In the example above, the sum_list function takes a list and computes the sum of its elements. The match statement evaluates lst. If the list is empty ([]), it returns 0. If the list contains elements, it splits the list into head (the first element) and tail (the rest of the list), summing the head with the recursive result of summing the tail.

Lists can also be constructed using the :: operator, also known as the cons operator. This operator adds an element to the front of a list:

```
let new_list = 1 :: [2; 3; 4]
```

This results in new_list being [1; 2; 3; 4].

More complex patterns can be matched to perform various operations on lists.

```
let rec remove_evens lst =
  match lst with
  | [] -> []
  | head :: tail ->
      if head mod 2 = 0 then remove_evens tail
      else head :: remove_evens tail
```

The remove_evens function processes a list and removes all even elements. The match statement checks if the head of the list is even using the modulus operator (mod) and accordingly decides whether to include it in the result.

Pattern matching also supports wildcard patterns, which are used when the value of the matched part is not of interest. Consider the following example:

```
let is_empty lst =
  match lst with
  | [] -> true
  | _ :: _ -> false
```

In this function, _ :: _ matches any non-empty list, effectively ignoring the actual contents.

Pattern matching with lists can also involve nested patterns:

```
let rec flatten lst =
  match lst with
  | [] -> []
  | head :: tail -> head @ flatten tail
```

Here, flatten is a function to convert a list of lists into a single list. The operator @ concatenates two lists. If lst is non-empty, head (a list itself) is concatenated with the flattened tail.

Pattern matching and lists can be further combined with guards for more selective operations:

```
let rec find_first_positive lst =
  match lst with
  | [] -> None
  | head :: tail when head > 0 -> Some head
  | _ :: tail -> find_first_positive tail
```

The find_first_positive function searches the list for the first positive number. If such a number is found, it returns Some head; otherwise, it continues searching.

When working with lists and pattern matching, it is also essential to leverage the standard library functions available in OCaml, such as List.map, List.fold_left, and List.filter which provide a higher-level abstraction for common operations.

```
let increment_all lst = List.map ((+) 1) lst

let sum_all lst = List.fold_left (+) 0 lst

let remove_negatives lst = List.filter ((>=) 0) lst
```

The use of List.map, List.fold_left, and List.filter can result in more concise and readable code compared to manual recursion and pattern matching.

Understanding the interplay between lists and pattern matching is essential for harnessing the full capabilities of OCaml for functional data manipulation. These constructs form the basis of numerous higher-order functions and algorithms used throughout OCaml programming.

5.2 Arrays and Mutable Data Structures

In OCaml, arrays are a fundamental mutable data structure that allows for efficient direct access and modification of elements. Arrays, unlike lists, provide constant time complexity for access and update operations due to their contiguous memory allocation. This section examines the declaration, manipulation, and utilization of arrays, as well as explores other mutable data structures available in OCaml.

An array in OCaml is declared and initialized using the Array.make function or with array literals. The Array.make function creates an array of a specified size, with all elements initialized to a given value:

```
let arr = Array.make 5 0;;
(* arr: int array = [|0; 0; 0; 0; 0|] *)
```

Alternatively, array literals provide a succinct way to declare and initialize arrays:

```
let arr = [|1; 2; 3; 4; 5|];;
(* arr: int array = [|1; 2; 3; 4; 5|] *)
```

Access to array elements is achieved using the .( ) operator:

```
let elem = arr.(2);;
(* elem: int = 3 *)
```

Modification of array elements follows the same syntax:

```
arr.(2) <- 10;;
(* arr: int array = [|1; 2; 10; 4; 5|] *)
```

To determine the length of an array, the Array.length function is used:

```
let length = Array.length arr;;
(* length: int = 5 *)
```

Arrays are part of the Array module, which includes various utility functions for array manipulation. For instance, Array.iter applies a function to each element:

```
Array.iter (fun x -> Printf.printf "%d " x) arr;;
(* Output: 1 2 10 4 5 *)
```

The Array.map function creates a new array by applying a function to each element of the original array:

```
let squared = Array.map (fun x -> x * x) arr;;
(* squared: int array = [|1; 4; 100; 16; 25|] *)
```

One significant aspect of arrays in OCaml is their mutability. This characteristic means that arrays allow in-place modification of their elements, which can be advantageous for certain applications that require frequent updates. However, this mutability requires careful handling to avoid unintended side effects, especially in concurrent or functional programming contexts.

In addition to arrays, OCaml also provides other mutable data structures such as references and mutable fields within records. References are single-element mutable containers that can store any type. They are declared using the ref keyword and accessed or modified using the ! operator and the := operator, respectively:

```
let x = ref 0;;
(* x: int ref = {contents = 0} *)

x := 5;;
(* x: int ref = {contents = 5} *)

let y = !x;;
(* y: int = 5 *)
```

Mutable fields within records are another form of mutable data structure. A record type with mutable fields can be defined using the mutable keyword. Modifying the field values is done using the <- operator:

```
type point = {
  mutable x: float;
  mutable y: float;
};;

let p = {x = 0.0; y = 0.0};;
(* p: point = {x = 0.; y = 0.} *)

p.x <- 1.0;;
(* p: point = {x = 1.0; y = 0.0} *)

p.y <- 2.0;;
(* p: point = {x = 1.0; y = 2.0} *)
```

Understanding the usage and implications of mutable data structures is crucial when designing efficient and effective OCaml programs. The choice between mutable and immutable data structures often depends on the specific requirements and constraints of the application. Mutable data structures can provide performance benefits through in-place updates, but they must be used judiciously to maintain code safety and readability.

5.3 Records and Field Access

Records in OCaml are a form of data structure that allows the grouping of related values, much like structs in C or objects in other programming languages. A record is defined by listing its fields, each paired with a specific type. To demonstrate their usage, let us first create a simple record type.

```
type person = {
    name : string;
    age : int;
    email : string;
}
```

In this example, we define a record type named person with three fields: name, age, and email. Each field is associated with a type, indicating the kind of data it can hold. Records in OCaml provide a convenient way to package related data into a single composite item.

To instantiate a person record, we can use the following syntax:

```
let john_doe = {
    name = "John Doe";
    age = 30;
    email = "john.doe@example.com";
}
```

Here, the john_doe record is created by supplying values for each of the fields defined in the person type. Each field value is specified using the syntax field_name = value, and the values are separated by semicolons.

Accessing the fields of a record can be done using the dot (.) notation:

```
let johns_name = john_doe.name;;
let johns_age = john_doe.age;;
let johns_email = john_doe.email;;
```

In this snippet, each field of the john_doe record is accessed individually and assigned to the corresponding variable. The use of . allows precise identification of the field in the record.

Updating fields within a record is a common operation. OCaml provides a concise syntax to create a new record instance with updated fields based on an existing one:

```
let older_john = { john_doe with age = 31 };;
```

Here, the older_john record is derived from john_doe with the age field updated to 31. The with keyword facilitates this succinct update, while the values of non-specified fields remain unchanged.

Pattern matching can also be employed with records to deconstruct them and access their fields more conveniently:

```
let display_person {name; age; email} =
    Printf.printf "Name: %s, Age: %d, Email: %s\n" name age email;;

display_person john_doe;;
```

In the function display_person, the record is decomposed into its fields directly in the parameter list using pattern matching. This method can simplify scenarios where multiple fields of a record need to be accessed at once.

Records are versatile data structures in OCaml, but they have more specialized uses. For example, they can be employed to create nested records, where a field itself can be a record type:

```
type address = {
    street : string;
    city : string;
    country : string;
}

type employee = {
    id : int;
    name : string;
    contact : address;
}

let emp = {
    id = 101;
    name = "Alice";
    contact = {
        street = "456 Maple St";
        city = "Wonderland";
        country = "Imagination";
    };
};;

let emp_city = emp.contact.city;;
```

In this setup, the contact field of the employee record is itself an address record. Accessing a nested field, such as the city of the contact address, follows the dot notation for each layer of nested fields.

For cases demanding optional fields within records, option types can be utilized. Optional fields can hold either a value or None, indicating the absence of a value:

```
type car = {
    make : string;
    model : string;
    year : int option;
}

let my_car = {
    make = "Tesla";
    model = "Model S";
    year = Some 2020;
}

let old_car = {
    make = "Ford";
    model = "T";
    year = None;
}

let print_car_year car =
    match car.year with
    | Some y -> Printf.printf "Year: %d\n" y
    | None -> Printf.printf "Year: Unspecified\n";;
```

In this example, the year field in the car record type can either be an integer enclosed within Some or None. The print_car_year function demonstrates how to handle optional fields using pattern matching, offering different actions based on the presence or absence of a value.

This capability to capture missing data succinctly within a well-defined structure is one of the strengths of using records with optional fields.

5.4 Variants and Tagged Unions

Variants and tagged unions are pivotal constructs within OCaml, enabling the creation of complex data types that can represent distinct possibilities and states within a program. The use of variants involves defining a type with several constructors, each potentially carrying different types of data. This allows for elegant and type-safe handling of situations where a variable can take on multiple forms.

To begin, consider a simple variant type representing a binary result, which can either be successful or fail:

```
type result =
  | Success
  | Failure of string
```

In this example, the result type has two constructors: Success and Failure. Success takes no additional data, whereas Failure holds a string, providing an error message.

The ability to pattern match on variant types is essential for utilizing these constructs effectively. Pattern matching allows the extraction of data and differentiation between constructors in a clean and concise manner:

```
let handle_result res =
  match res with
  | Success -> print_endline "Operation was successful."
  | Failure msg -> print_endline ("Operation failed with error: " ^ msg)
```

Determining the behavior based on the constructor is achieved through the match expression. Here, the handle_result function prints an appropriate message depending on whether res is Success or Failure.

Variants can also store different types of data, not just single types. For instance, consider a variant representing a geometric shape:

```
type shape =
  | Circle of float
  | Rectangle of float * float
  | Triangle of float * float * float
```

The shape type has three constructors: Circle, which holds a float representing the radius, Rectangle, which holds two floats representing the width and height, and Triangle, which holds three floats representing the lengths of its sides. The ability to contain diverse data within each constructor demonstrates the flexibility of variants.

When working with variants, calculating properties or creating utility functions becomes straightforward due to pattern matching:

```
let area s =
  match s with
  | Circle r -> 3.14159265358979 *. r *. r
  | Rectangle (w, h) -> w *. h
  | Triangle (a, b, c) ->
      let s = (a +. b +. c) /. 2.0 in
      sqrt (s *. (s -. a) *. (s -. b) *. (s -. c))
```

In this area function, the shape is matched against its constructors, and the appropriate formula is applied. The expression sqrt (s *. (s -. a) *. (s -. b) *. (s -. c)) computes the area of the triangle using Heron's formula.

Variants are inherently recursive, enabling the definition of more complex data structures such as trees. For example, a binary tree that stores integers can be defined as:

```
type int_tree =
```

```
  | Empty
  | Node of int * int_tree * int_tree
```

This int_tree type has two constructors: Empty, representing an empty tree, and Node, which stores an integer value and two subtrees. Functions operating on this tree can be similarly defined with pattern matching:

```
let rec sum_tree t =
  match t with
  | Empty -> 0
  | Node (v, left, right) -> v + (sum_tree left) + (sum_tree right)
```

The sum_tree function recursively computes the sum of all values in the tree, effectively applying pattern matching to process each node.

Tagged unions, also known as algebraic data types (ADTs), extend the concept of variants, allowing for even greater flexibility by enabling combination of multiple types. OCaml does not have a distinct construct named tagged unions, but the capability is embedded within its variant types. They are instrumental when encoding data that may possess multiple, heterogeneous forms.

An example involving variant types to model a message passing system can illustrate this:

```
type message =
  | Text of string
  | Image of string * int * int
  | Video of string * float
```

In this message type, Text holds a string for text messages, Image holds a filename and dimensions, while Video includes a filename and duration. The variant constructors effectively tag the data, signifying their type and aiding pattern matching:

```
let print_message msg =
  match msg with
  | Text s -> print_endline ("Text: " ^ s)
  | Image (filename, w, h) -> print_endline ("Image: " ^ filename ^ " (" ^
      string_of_int w ^ "x" ^ string_of_int h ^ ")")
  | Video (filename, duration) -> print_endline ("Video: " ^ filename ^ " (" ^
      string_of_float duration ^ "s)")
```

In the print_message function, the message is decomposed based on its type, providing the appropriate output. This approach ensures type safety and preserves the integrity of each data form.

Understanding and effectively employing variants and tagged unions is fundamental for managing diverse data structures in OCaml. Mastery of these constructs leads to clearer, more maintainable, and type-safe code, essential for advanced OCaml programming techniques.

5.5 Dictionaries and Hash Tables

Dictionaries in OCaml are implemented using hash tables. These hash tables provide an efficient means of storing key-value pairs and offer constant time complexity, O(1), for average case look-up, insert, and delete operations. Hash tables are integral in scenarios where quick access to data based on unique keys is required.

To utilize hash tables in OCaml, it is necessary to include the standard library module Hashtbl. This module provides a comprehensive suite of functions for creating and manipulating hash tables.

Below, we demonstrate how to create a hash table and perform fundamental operations like adding, looking up, and removing key-value pairs.

```
(* Create a new hash table *)
let phone_book = Hashtbl.create 10;;
```

The Hashtbl.create function initializes a new, empty hash table. The argument 10 indicates the initial size of the table, though the table may resize dynamically.

To add key-value pairs to the hash table, use the Hashtbl.add function. This function takes three arguments: the hash table, the key, and the value.

```
(* Add entries to the phone book *)
Hashtbl.add phone_book "Alice" "555-1234";;
Hashtbl.add phone_book "Bob" "555-5678";;
Hashtbl.add phone_book "Charlie" "555-8765";;
```

Retrieve a value associated with a key using the Hashtbl.find function. If the key is not present in the hash table, the Not_found exception is raised.

```
(* Look up a phone number *)
let number = Hashtbl.find phone_book "Alice";;
```

To handle the situation where a key might not exist, you can use exception handling.

```
(* Safe lookup with exception handling *)
let safe_lookup key hashtable =
```

```
  try
    Some (Hashtbl.find hashtable key)
  with
    Not_found -> None
;;
```

Removing a key-value pair is straightforward with the Hashtbl.remove function.

```
(* Remove an entry from the phone book *)
Hashtbl.remove phone_book "Charlie";;
```

The Hashtbl module also provides other useful functions, such as Hashtbl.mem to check for the existence of a key, Hashtbl.iter to apply a function to all key-value pairs, and Hashtbl.fold to aggregate results from the hash table.

Hashtbl.mem is used to determine if a key exists in the hash table:

```
(* Check if a key exists *)
let exists = Hashtbl.mem phone_book "Bob";;
```

To iterate over all key-value pairs, use Hashtbl.iter:

```
(* Iterate over all entries in the phone book *)
Hashtbl.iter (fun key value ->
  Printf.printf "%s: %s\n" key value
) phone_book;;
```

Finally, Hashtbl.fold allows you to accumulate results from the hash table into a single value:

```
(* Create a list of all keys in the phone book *)
let keys = Hashtbl.fold (fun key _ acc -> key :: acc) phone_book [];;
```

The effectiveness of hash tables depends heavily on the quality of the hash function used. OCaml's standard library provides a satisfactory default hashing mechanism through Hashtbl.hash. However, for custom types, you may need to define your own hash and equality functions to ensure proper distribution and access.

Consider a scenario where points are defined in a two-dimensional space, and you want to store these points in a hash table:

```
type point = { x: int; y: int };;

module PointHash =
struct
  type t = point
  let equal p1 p2 = (p1.x = p2.x) && (p1.y = p2.y)
  let hash p = Hashtbl.hash (p.x, p.y)
end;;
```

```
module PointHashtbl = Hashtbl.Make(PointHash);;

let points_table = PointHashtbl.create 10;;
```

This example demonstrates creating a module that defines a custom hashing strategy by implementing the Hashtbl.HashedType interface. The equal function ensures that two points are compared based on their coordinates, and the hash function computes the hash value by combining the coordinates.

Hash tables are a versatile and high-performance data structure well-suited for various applications requiring quick lookup and modification of key-value pairs. Beyond the basic functionalities, their efficiency in managing large volumes of data makes them essential in numerous computational tasks.

5.6 Sets and Maps

Sets and maps are fundamental data structures in OCaml that facilitate efficient data organization and retrieval. OCaml provides robust modules for their implementation, primarily under the Set and Map modules. These modules are parameterized over a type, harnessing the power of OCaml's functional programming paradigm.

Sets

In OCaml, a set is a collection of elements where each element is unique. Sets are implemented as balanced binary trees, ensuring logarithmic access times for insertion, deletion, and membership testing.

To utilize sets, the Set module must first be opened or referenced. Sets are functorized with a module that defines the type of elements stored in the set and provides comparison functions.

Here is an example to illustrate the use of sets with integers:

```
module IntSet = Set.Make(struct
  type t = int
  let compare = compare
end)
```

This snippet creates a module IntSet specialized for integer elements. Basic operations can now be performed using this module:

```
// Create an empty set
let empty_set = IntSet.empty
```

```
// Add elements to the set
let set1 = IntSet.add 3 empty_set
let set2 = IntSet.add 5 set1
```

Sets also support operations like union, intersection, and difference:

```
// Union of two sets
let union_set = IntSet.union set1 set2

// Intersection of two sets
let inter_set = IntSet.inter set1 set2

// Difference of two sets
let diff_set = IntSet.diff set2 set1
```

Membership testing and iteration over set elements:

```
// Membership testing
let is_member = IntSet.mem 3 set2 // Returns: true

// Iteration: Printing the elements of a set
IntSet.iter (Printf.printf "%d\n") set2
```

Maps

Maps in OCaml consist of key-value pairs, where each key is unique. Like sets, maps are implemented using balanced binary trees, ensuring efficient access.

To use maps, the Map module must be properly parameterized. Let's see an example of maps where integer keys map to string values:

```
module IntMap = Map.Make(struct
  type t = int
  let compare = compare
end)
```

Basic map operations include insertion, lookup, and deletion of key-value pairs:

```
// Create an empty map
let empty_map = IntMap.empty

// Add key-value pairs to the map
let map1 = IntMap.add 1 "one" empty_map
let map2 = IntMap.add 2 "two" map1
```

Lookup and removing key-value pairs from maps:

```
// Find a value by key
let value = IntMap.find 1 map2 // Returns: "one"

// Remove a key-value pair
let map_without_one = IntMap.remove 1 map2
```

Maps also support iterating over all key-value pairs, as well as transformations:

```
// Iteration: Printing all key-value pairs
IntMap.iter (fun k v -> Printf.printf "%d: %s\n" k v) map2

// Transformation: Applying a function to all values
let incremented_map = IntMap.map (fun v -> v ^ " incremented") map2
```

Another useful function is fold, which iterates over the map, accumulating a result:

```
let sum_of_keys_and_lengths =
  IntMap.fold (fun k v acc -> acc + k + String.length v) map2 0
```

This function sums the keys and the lengths of all string values in map2.

Combining sets and maps can also be advantageous. For example, we could keep track of sets of keys within a map:

```
module IntSetMap = Map.Make(struct
  type t = int
  let compare = compare
end)

let map_of_sets = IntSetMap.add 1 (IntSet.add 1 IntSet.empty) IntSetMap.empty
```

In this scenario, map_of_sets contains sets of integers as values indexed by integer keys, providing a powerful structure for more complex data organization scenarios.

Efficient utilization of sets and maps can greatly optimize performance, especially in computation-heavy tasks where frequent lookups, insertions, and deletions are necessary.

5.7 Custom Data Types

Custom data types in OCaml provide a robust way to model and represent complex data structures. By defining new data types, we can encapsulate specific properties and behaviors that are critical for our programs. Custom data types in OCaml are primarily created using the type keyword. These types can represent simple enumeration, product types (tuples), or sum types (variants).

Enumeration Types: These are the simplest form of custom data types. They define a type by listing its possible values. For example, consider an enumeration type for days of the week:

```
type day =
  | Monday
  | Tuesday
  | Wednesday
  | Thursday
  | Friday
  | Saturday
  | Sunday
```

Here, the day type can have one of seven values: Monday, Tuesday, Wednesday, Thursday, Friday, Saturday, or Sunday. This is useful for creating readable and concise code that works with specific sets of values.

Product Types (Tuples): Product types allow us to define types that can hold multiple values, often of different types. This corresponds to the notion of tuples. For example, to represent a 2D point with floating-point coordinates, we can define:

```
type point2D = float * float
```

We can also create more complex product types that include named fields using records. This improves code readability and type safety. For instance:

```
type point3D = {
  x: float;
  y: float;
  z: float;
}
```

Here, point3D contains three fields x, y, and z, all of which are of type float. To create a point3D instance and access its fields, we can do:

```
let pt = {x = 1.0; y = 2.0; z = 3.0};;
let x_coord = pt.x;;
```

Sum Types (Variants): Sum types, or variants, define types that can have different forms, each with its own set of associated values. This is one of the most powerful features in OCaml for defining complex data types. For example, consider a type to represent a shape, which could be a circle or a rectangle:

```
type shape =
  | Circle of float (* radius *)
  | Rectangle of float * float (* width, height *)
```

Here, shape can be a Circle with a radius (a float) or a Rectangle with width and height (both are floats). This type allows us to define functions that can operate on different shapes:

```
let area s =
  match s with
  | Circle r -> 3.1415 *. r *. r
  | Rectangle (w, h) -> w *. h;;
```

Pattern matching is used here to distinguish whether the shape is a Circle or a Rectangle and calculate the area accordingly.

Polymorphic Variants: OCaml also supports polymorphic variants, which provide greater flexibility. Polymorphic variants do not require pre-declaration before use, but they must be used consistently. Here is a comparable example using polymorphic variants:

```
let area = function
  | `Circle r -> 3.1415 *. r *. r
  | `Rectangle (w, h) -> w *. h;;
```

In this example, backticks (`) are used to define the polymorphic variant constructors.

Recursive Types: Custom data types can be recursive, allowing for the creation of self-referential structures like linked lists and trees. For instance, a binary tree can be defined as:

```
type 'a binary_tree =
  | Empty
  | Node of 'a * 'a binary_tree * 'a binary_tree
```

This type defines a binary tree where each node contains a value of type 'a, and has two children which are also binary trees. The tree can either be Empty or a Node containing a value and two subtrees.

To operate on this binary tree, consider a function to calculate its depth:

```
let rec depth tree =
  match tree with
  | Empty -> 0
  | Node (_, left, right) ->
    1 + max (depth left) (depth right);;
```

In this function, we recursively determine the depth of the left and right subtrees and return the maximum of the two, plus one for the current node depth.

Understanding custom data types in OCaml is crucial for creating efficient and readable code. They allow the programmer to precisely model the problem domain and leverage the power of pattern matching for concise and clear control structures.

5.8 Tree Data Structures

Tree data structures are hierarchical structures widely used for various applications such as representing hierarchical data, managing sorted lists of data, facilitating quick search, insertion, and deletion operations, and more. This section delves into the fundamentals of trees, their implementation in OCaml, and the various types of trees including binary trees, binary search trees, and more complex forms such as AVL trees and red-black trees.

A tree consists of nodes with a root node serving as the entry point. Each node can have zero or more child nodes, and nodes with no children are called leaf nodes. A typical tree structure has the following characteristics:

- **Root:** The topmost node in the tree.
- **Node:** An element containing a value and references to its children.
- **Edge:** The connection between a parent node and a child node.
- **Leaf:** A node with no children.
- **Subtree:** A tree consisting of a node and its descendants.
- **Depth:** The number of edges from the root to the node.
- **Height:** The number of edges from the node to the deepest leaf.

Binary Trees

A binary tree is a tree structure where each node has at most two children referred to as the left child and the right child. In OCaml, a binary tree can be represented using the following type definition:

```
type 'a binary_tree =
  | Empty
  | Node of 'a * 'a binary_tree * 'a binary_tree
```

Here is how you would create a simple binary tree with integers:

```
let tree =
  Node (1,
        Node (2, Empty, Empty),
        Node (3, Empty, Empty))
```

This OCaml code creates a binary tree where the root node has the value 1, its left child has the value 2, and its right child has the value 3.

Tree Traversal

Traversal refers to the process of visiting all the nodes in a tree in a specific order. The main types of traversals are in-order, pre-order, and post-order.

In-order traversal visits nodes in the left subtree, then the current node, and finally the nodes in the right subtree. The algorithm can be implemented in OCaml as follows:

```
let rec in_order_traversal tree =
  match tree with
  | Empty -> []
  | Node (value, left, right) ->
      (in_order_traversal left) @ [value] @ (in_order_traversal right)
```

Pre-order traversal visits the current node before visiting its left and right subtrees:

```
let rec pre_order_traversal tree =
  match tree with
  | Empty -> []
  | Node (value, left, right) ->
      [value] @ (pre_order_traversal left) @ (pre_order_traversal right)
```

Post-order traversal visits the nodes in the left subtree, then those in the right subtree, and finally the current node:

```
let rec post_order_traversal tree =
  match tree with
  | Empty -> []
  | Node (value, left, right) ->
      (post_order_traversal left) @ (post_order_traversal right) @ [value]
```

Binary Search Trees (BST)

Binary Search Trees (BST) are a special kind of binary tree that maintains the order of elements such that for any given node, the elements in the left subtree are less than the node's value, and the elements in the right subtree are greater. This property makes BSTs particularly useful for efficient search, insertion, and deletion operations.

Search Operation for a value in a BST can be implemented as follows:

```
let rec search_bst value tree =
  match tree with
  | Empty -> false
  | Node (v, left, right) ->
      if value = v then
        true
      else if value < v then
```

```
    search_bst value left
  else
    search_bst value right
```

The search operation traverses the tree, comparing the desired value with the current node's value and choosing the appropriate subtree to continue the search.

Insertion Operation for adding a value to a BST:

```
let rec insert_bst value tree =
  match tree with
  | Empty -> Node (value, Empty, Empty)
  | Node (v, left, right) ->
      if value < v then
        Node (v, insert_bst value left, right)
      else
        Node (v, left, insert_bst value right)
```

Insertion involves finding the correct location in the tree such that the BST properties are maintained after adding the new value.

Balancing Trees

Balanced trees are critical for ensuring that the operations such as search, insertion, and deletion maintain efficient time complexity. Unbalanced trees can degenerate to linked lists in the worst-case scenarios. AVL trees and red-black trees are common self-balancing binary search trees.

AVL Trees (named after their inventors Adelson-Velsky and Landis) maintain a balance factor for each node, which is the difference in height between the left and right subtrees. The tree rebalances itself through rotations whenever a node's balance factor becomes greater than 1 or less than -1.

The following represents a simplified insertion algorithm for AVL trees using OCaml:

```
type 'a avl_tree =
  | Empty
  | Node of 'a * 'a avl_tree * 'a avl_tree * int (* Balance factor *)

let height tree =
  match tree with
  | Empty -> 0
  | Node (_, _, _, h) -> h

let create_node value left right =
  let h = max (height left) (height right) + 1 in
  Node (value, left, right, h)
```

This type definition includes a height/balance factor for each node. The create_node function calculates the height of a newly created node. Details on rotations and balancing logic would be further elaborated to ensure AVL tree properties are maintained.

Red-Black Trees employ an additional property of coloring nodes (either red or black) and enforce properties to maintain balance. Each node stores its color along with its value and children. The balancing operations involve rotations and color flips.

```
type color = Red | Black

type 'a rb_tree =
  | Empty
  | Node of color * 'a * 'a rb_tree * 'a rb_tree

let make_black = function
  | Empty -> Empty
  | Node (_, v, l, r) -> Node (Black, v, l, r)
```

Here, the rb_tree type embodies the color as part of the node definition. operations for inserting and ensuring the red-black properties would include re-adjustments through rotations and re-coloring to preserve the properties of the red-black tree.

5.9 Graph Data Structures

In this section, we will delve into the representation, construction, and manipulation of graph data structures in OCaml. Graphs are versatile structures used to model various relationships and processes in computer science, such as networks, social connections, and dependency trees. We will cover directed, undirected, weighted, and unweighted graphs, and explore essential operations such as traversal, pathfinding, and cycle detection.

Graphs in OCaml can be represented using adjacency lists or adjacency matrices. Each representation has its advantages and use-cases.

1. Adjacency List Representation

An adjacency list is a common way of representing a graph, where each node stores a list of adjacent nodes. This representation is space-efficient for sparse graphs. In OCaml, adjacency lists can be implemented using list or Map modules. Here is an example implementation using lists:

```
type 'a graph = ('a * 'a list) list
```

```
(* Create an empty graph *)
let empty_graph : 'a graph = []

(* Add a vertex to the graph *)
let add_vertex v g =
  if List.exists (fun (x, _) -> x = v) g then g
  else (v, []) :: g

(* Add an edge to the graph *)
let add_edge v1 v2 g =
  List.map (fun (x, l) -> if x = v1 then (x, v2 :: l) else (x, l)) g

(* Example usage *)
let g = add_vertex 1 (add_vertex 2 (add_vertex 3 empty_graph))
let g = add_edge 1 2 g
let g = add_edge 2 3 g
```

In this example, the type 'a graph defines an adjacency list where each vertex is associated with a list of connected vertices. Operations for adding vertices and edges are straightforward, using list manipulations.

2. Adjacency Matrix Representation

An adjacency matrix is a two-dimensional array where the element at row i and column j is non-zero if there is an edge from vertex i to vertex j. This representation is suitable for dense graphs. In OCaml, adjacency matrices can be implemented using the Array and Matrix modules.

```
type graph = int array array

(* Create an empty graph with n vertices *)
let create_graph n =
  Array.make_matrix n n 0

(* Add an edge to the graph *)
let add_edge g v1 v2 =
  g.(v1).(v2) <- 1

(* Example usage *)
let g = create_graph 3
let () = add_edge g 0 1
let () = add_edge g 1 2
```

Here, the type graph is defined as a 2D array. The create_graph function initializes an empty graph, while add_edge modifies the matrix to reflect the graph's edges.

Traversal Algorithms

Graph traversal is a fundamental operation in graph theory. The most common traversal algorithms are Depth-First Search (DFS) and Breadth-First Search (BFS). Below are implementations of both in OCaml:

```
(* Depth-First Search (DFS) *)
let dfs graph start =
  let rec dfs_rec visited stack =
    match stack with
    | [] -> List.rev visited
    | v :: rest ->
        if List.mem v visited then
          dfs_rec visited rest
        else
          let neighbors = List.assoc v graph in
          dfs_rec (v :: visited) (neighbors @ rest)
  in
  dfs_rec [] [start]

(* Example usage *)
let g = [(1, [2; 3]); (2, [4]); (3, [4]); (4, [])]
let result = dfs g 1
```

The above code demonstrates a DFS implementation for an adjacency list, where the dfs_rec function explores nodes recursively, maintaining a stack of nodes to visit and a list of visited nodes.

```
(* Breadth-First Search (BFS) *)
let bfs graph start =
  let rec bfs_rec visited queue =
    match queue with
    | [] -> List.rev visited
    | v :: rest ->
        if List.mem v visited then
          bfs_rec visited rest
        else
          let neighbors = List.assoc v graph in
          bfs_rec (v :: visited) (rest @ neighbors)
  in
  bfs_rec [] [start]

(* Example usage *)
let g = [(1, [2; 3]); (2, [4]); (3, [4]); (4, [])]
let result = bfs g 1
```

For BFS, the bfs_rec function processes nodes in a queue (FIFO) manner. This ensures that nodes are visited in level-order.

Pathfinding

Pathfinding algorithms aim to find a path between two vertices in a graph. One common algorithm is Dijkstra's algorithm for shortest paths in weighted graphs. Below is a straightforward implementation using a priority queue represented by a heap:

```
module PQ = Heap.Make(struct
  type t = int * int (* (distance, vertex) *)
  let compare (d1, _) (d2, _) = compare d1 d2
end)

let dijkstra graph src =
  let dist = Hashtbl.create (List.length graph) in
```

```
  List.iter (fun (v, _) -> Hashtbl.add dist v max_int) graph;
  Hashtbl.replace dist src 0;
  let pq = PQ.singleton (0, src) in
  let rec aux pq =
    if PQ.is_empty pq then ()
    else
      let (d, u) = PQ.extract_min pq in
      let neighbors = List.assoc u graph in
      List.iter (fun (v, weight) ->
        let alt = d + weight in
        if alt < Hashtbl.find dist v then
          (Hashtbl.replace dist v alt;
           PQ.add pq (alt, v))
      ) neighbors;
      aux pq
  in
  aux pq;
  dist
```

In this example, the dijkstra function utilizes a priority queue (PQ) to keep track of the minimal distances as it explores the graph. The distance table is updated whenever a shorter path is found.

Cycle Detection

Detecting cycles in graphs is crucial for various applications like dependency resolution and scheduling. A common method for cycle detection in directed graphs is through Depth-First Search (DFS) with recursion stack bookkeeping.

```
(* Detect cycle in a graph *)
let has_cycle graph =
  let rec visit visited rec_stack v =
    if List.mem v rec_stack then true
    else if List.mem v visited then false
    else
      let neighbors = List.assoc v graph in
      List.fold_left (fun acc neighbor -> acc || visit (v :: visited) (v :: rec_stack)
            neighbor) false neighbors
  in
  List.exists (fun (v, _) -> visit [] [] v) graph

(* Example usage *)
let g = [(1, [2]); (2, [3]); (3, [1])]
let result = has_cycle g (* returns true *)
```

In this snippet, has_cycle recursively visits each node, tracking both visited nodes and the recursion stack to detect cycles.

Efficient use of graph data structures requires understanding the context in which they are deployed. Sparse graphs benefit from adjacency list representations, while dense graphs may require adjacency matrices. Ensuring efficient traversal, pathfinding, and cycle detection is paramount for many applications, from networking to resource management.

5.10 Using Data Structures for Efficiency

Efficient utilization of data structures is pivotal in OCaml programming to enhance the performance of applications. This section provides an in-depth examination of various data structures and methodologies to leverage them for optimal performance.

The selection of a data structure significantly influences the complexity of operations such as insertion, deletion, search, and iteration. OCaml offers a plethora of efficient data structures, each suited for distinct scenarios. This section aims to facilitate a comprehensive understanding of choosing and implementing the appropriate data structure to achieve high efficiency.

Time Complexity Considerations

Understanding the time complexity of operations is essential. For example, lists have $\mathcal{O}(1)$ complexity for prepend operations but $\mathcal{O}(n)$ for access and append operations. Conversely, arrays provide $\mathcal{O}(1)$ access time but $\mathcal{O}(n)$ for insertion and deletion at arbitrary positions. The table below summarizes the average time complexities of common operations for lists and arrays.

Operation	Lists	Arrays
Access	$\mathcal{O}(n)$	$\mathcal{O}(1)$
Prepend	$\mathcal{O}(1)$	$\mathcal{O}(n)$
Append	$\mathcal{O}(n)$	$\mathcal{O}(n)$
Insert/Delete	$\mathcal{O}(n)$	$\mathcal{O}(n)$

Lists: Fast Prepend with Lazy Evaluation

OCaml lists offer efficient prepend operations, essential for scenarios requiring frequent element addition at the head of the list.

```
let lst = 1 :: [2; 3; 4]
```

Pattern matching can optimize operations by handling elements selectively.

```
let rec sum_list lst =
  match lst with
  | [] -> 0
  | head :: tail -> head + sum_list tail
```

Arrays: Efficient Random Access

Arrays facilitate efficient random access and in-place updates, beneficial for performance-intensive applications such as numerical simulations.

```
let arr = [|1; 2; 3; 4|]
arr.(2) <- 42
```

Hash Tables: Average $\mathcal{O}(1)$ Complexity

For associative collections, hash tables provide average $\mathcal{O}(1)$ time complexity for inserts, deletes, and lookups.

```
let htbl = Hashtbl.create 10;;
Hashtbl.add htbl "key" "value";;
Hashtbl.find htbl "key";;
```

```
- : string = "value"
```

Sets and Maps

OCaml's Set and Map modules store unique elements and key-value pairs respectively, implemented as balanced binary trees.

```
module StringSet = Set.Make(String);;
let set = StringSet.add "hello" StringSet.empty;;
StringSet.mem "hello" set;;
```

```
- : bool = true
```

```
module StringMap = Map.Make(String);;
let map = StringMap.add "key1" "value1" StringMap.empty;;
StringMap.find "key1" map;;
```

```
- : string = "value1"
```

Custom Data Types

User-defined data types and abstract data types (ADTs) allow for tailored efficiency based on specific use cases.

```
type 'a tree =
  | Empty
  | Node of 'a * 'a tree * 'a tree

let rec insert x t =
  match t with
  | Empty -> Node(x, Empty, Empty)
  | Node(y, left, right) ->
    if x < y then Node(y, insert x left, right)
    else Node(y, left, insert x right)
```

Algorithm Selection for Optimal Performance

The choice of algorithms often accompanies data structure selection for performance efficiency. The algorithm2e package enables formal algorithmic representation.

Algorithm 1: Selection Sort

```
Data: lst - List of integers
Result: Sorted list
begin
    while unsorted elements remain do
        Find the smallest element;
        Move it to the result list;
    end
end
```

Integrating data structures with efficient algorithms ensures streamlined performance. Selecting and implementing appropriate data structures directly impacts the efficiency and scalability of programs written in OCaml.

Chapter 6

Modules and Functors

This chapter explores OCaml's modular programming capabilities, starting with an introduction to modules and their signatures. We will delve into abstract data types, basic and advanced usage of functors, and parameterized modules. Additional topics include module types and constraints, nested modules, and the organization of compilation units. The chapter concludes with best practices for effectively using modules and functors to create modular, reusable, and maintainable code.

6.1 Introduction to Modules

An OCaml module is a robust construct that encapsulates a collection of related values, types, functions, and even other modules. Modules are fundamental in structuring large OCaml programs, promoting code reuse, and enhancing maintainability. Modules serve as namespaces, preventing naming conflicts and aiding in the logical grouping of entities.

Consider a basic module in OCaml. The module declaration employs the module keyword followed by the module name and an assignment to a struct that contains the encapsulated entities. The module's name must start with an uppercase letter.

```
module MathUtilities = struct
  let pi = 3.14159
  let square x = x *. x
  let cube x = x *. x *. x
```

```
end
```

In the above example, the module MathUtilities contains a floating-point constant pi and two functions, square and cube. These module components are accessed using dot notation:

```
let area_of_circle r = MathUtilities.pi *. MathUtilities.square r
```

```
area_of_circle 1.0;;
- : float = 3.14159
```

This illustrative example highlights a fundamental feature of modules: they enable grouping related definitions, which can then be collectively referenced through the module name. The dot notation serves as a scope operator, indicating that pi and square are members of MathUtilities.

Modules can also have nested modules, allowing for further organization. Consider the enhancement of the above example with submodules for specific mathematical operations.

```
module AdvancedMath = struct
  module Trigonometry = struct
    let sin x = (* implementation of sine, possibly involving approximations or series
        expansion *)
    let cos x = (* implementation of cosine *)
  end

  module Algebra = struct
    let solve_quadratic a b c =
      let discriminant = b *. b -. 4.0 *. a *. c in
      ((-.b +. sqrt(discriminant)) /. (2.0 *. a),
       (-.b -. sqrt(discriminant)) /. (2.0 *. a))
  end
end
```

Accessing nested modules follows similar principles:

```
let root1, root2 = AdvancedMath.Algebra.solve_quadratic 1.0 (-3.0) 2.0
```

```
root1, root2;;
- : float * float = (2.0, 1.0)
```

Module types, or signatures, are abstractions that specify which definitions within a module are publicly accessible. Signatures are defined using the sig keyword and can be applied to modules using the :> operator to enforce encapsulation. For the previous example, we can define a signature for the MathUtilities module:

```
module type MATH_UTILITIES_SIG = sig
  val pi : float
  val square : float -> float
  val cube : float -> float
end
```

To ensure that MathUtilities conforms to this signature, the with keyword is used as follows:

```
module MathUtilities : MATH_UTILITIES_SIG = struct
  let pi = 3.14159
  let square x = x *. x
  let cube x = x *. x *. x
end
```

The signature MATH_UTILITIES_SIG dictates that MathUtilities must contain a pi value and square and cube functions with specified types.

Encapsulation is further demonstrated with abstract data types (ADTs), where the type definitions within a module are hidden behind a signature. Consider a stack module where the underlying representation of the stack remains opaque:

```
module type STACK_SIG = sig
  type 'a stack
  val empty : 'a stack
  val push : 'a -> 'a stack -> 'a stack
  val pop : 'a stack -> ('a * 'a stack) option
end

module Stack : STACK_SIG = struct
  type 'a stack = 'a list
  let empty = []
  let push x st = x :: st
  let pop = function
    | [] -> None
    | x :: st -> Some (x, st)
end
```

Here, the stack type is defined as a list internally, but the external module users are unaware of this implementation detail due to the signature.

Using modules, signatures, nested modules, and ADTs allows OCaml programs to be structured logically, promotes code reuse, and enhances both security and maintainability by managing visibility and exposure of module internals effectively.

6.2 Module Signatures

Module signatures in OCaml define the interface of a module, specifying the types, values, and submodules that a module must implement. They are akin to the type signatures for functions but apply at the module level. Signatures enable abstraction, hiding implementation details while exposing essential components to the users of the module. The primary keyword used for defining a signature is sig.

A simple module signature might look like this:

```
module type StackSig = sig
  type 'a stack
  val empty : 'a stack
  val push : 'a -> 'a stack -> 'a stack
  val pop : 'a stack -> 'a stack
  val top : 'a stack -> 'a option
  val is_empty : 'a stack -> bool
end
```

In the StackSig signature, we define a type 'a stack and several associated functions to manipulate the stack. Each element's type is specified, providing a clear contract that any module implementing this signature must follow.

To implement a module that matches this signature, the module must provide concrete definitions for the type and functions specified:

```
module ListStack : StackSig = struct
  type 'a stack = 'a list
  let empty = []
  let push x stack = x :: stack
  let pop = function
    | [] -> failwith "Empty stack"
    | _ :: xs -> xs
  let top = function
    | [] -> None
    | x :: _ -> Some x
  let is_empty stack = stack = []
end
```

Here, ListStack conforms to the StackSig signature. The type 'a stack is defined as a list of 'a, and all functions are implemented accordingly. This clear definition and implementation ensure that users of ListStack can rely on its behavior as described by StackSig without concern for its internal workings.

Signatures and Type Abstraction

One of the key features of module signatures is type abstraction. By hiding the actual type implementation within a module, we can create more abstract and flexible code. For instance, in the previous example, the users of StackSig do not need to know that 'a stack is implemented as a list. This allows for different implementations of the stack without altering the interface.

We can further illustrate type abstraction with another implementation of StackSig using a different data structure:

```
module ArrayStack : StackSig = struct
  type 'a stack = {
    mutable arr : 'a array;
    mutable top : int;
  }
  let empty = { arr = [||]; top = -1 }
  let push x stack =
    let len = Array.length stack.arr in
    if stack.top + 1 >= len then (
      let new_len = max 2 (len * 2) in
      let new_arr = Array.make new_len x in
      Array.blit stack.arr 0 new_arr 0 len;
      stack.arr <- new_arr;
    );
    stack.top <- stack.top + 1;
    stack.arr.(stack.top) <- x;
    stack
  let pop stack =
    if stack.top < 0 then failwith "Empty stack"
    else (
      stack.top <- stack.top - 1;
      stack
    )
  let top stack =
    if stack.top < 0 then None
    else Some stack.arr.(stack.top)
  let is_empty stack = stack.top < 0
end
```

In this implementation, 'a stack is an array-based stack, demonstrating the flexibility and power of using module signatures in OCaml to abstract data types. Users can switch from ListStack to ArrayStack without any changes to the code that depends on StackSig.

Enforcing Module Signatures

When a module specifies that it adheres to a certain signature using the module ... : ... = struct ... end syntax, the OCaml compiler enforces this conformity. If a module does not provide all the types and values required by the signature, or if it provides them with incorrect types, the compiler will emit an error.

For example, attempting to implement StackSig without defining the push function will result in a compile-time error:

```
module InvalidStack : StackSig = struct
  type 'a stack = 'a list
```

```
  let empty = []
  let pop = function
    | [] -> failwith "Empty stack"
    | _ :: xs -> xs
  let top = function
    | [] -> None
    | x :: _ -> Some x
  let is_empty stack = stack = []
end
```

Compilation output:

```
Error: The implementation InvalidStack does not match the interface StackSig:
       The value 'push' is required but not provided
```

Including the push function in the implementation rectifies the error, ensuring that the module correctly conforms to the signature specified by StackSig.

By defining, enforcing, and abstracting module signatures, OCaml allows developers to create powerful and flexible modular programs.

6.3 Abstract Data Types

Abstract Data Types (ADTs) in OCaml play a pivotal role in enabling you to hide implementation details while exposing only the essential interface. This practice is crucial for creating robust, modular, and reusable code. By using abstract data types, you can enforce invariants and control how data is manipulated, fostering code reliability and maintainability.

When defining a module, the interface exposed is called its signature, and it defines what is visible to the users of the module. The abstract aspect comes from hiding the concrete implementation of the type within the module, exposing only the operations allowed on that type.

Here is a basic example to illustrate the concept. Consider an abstract data type for a simple stack:

```
module type Stack = sig
  type 'a t
  exception Empty
  val create : unit -> 'a t
  val push : 'a -> 'a t -> 'a t
  val pop : 'a t -> 'a
  val is_empty : 'a t -> bool
end
```

In this signature, type 'a t is the abstract type of stacks containing elements of type 'a. Although its implementation is hidden, users can see the operations that can be performed on stacks – creating a stack, pushing an element, popping an element, and checking if the stack is empty. The exception Empty is used to signal an attempt to pop from an empty stack.

Let's implement the above interface using a list. Here is how the implementation might look:

```
module ListStack : Stack = struct
  type 'a t = 'a list
  exception Empty

  let create () = []
  let push x s = x :: s
  let pop = function
    | [] -> raise Empty
    | x :: xs -> x
  let is_empty s = (s = [])
end
```

In this implementation, 'a t is concretely defined as 'a list, but this detail is hidden from the users of the ListStack module. They interact with stacks through the functions defined in the Stack signature.

Users of the ListStack module can create stacks and manipulate them without knowing that stacks are implemented as lists:

```
let s = ListStack.create ();;
let s = ListStack.push 1 s;;
let s = ListStack.push 2 s;;
let _ = ListStack.pop s;;
```

The concrete type of s is hidden; users can only operate on it via the methods provided by the signature.

Abstracting the data types offers several advantages:

- **Encapsulation**: The internal representation of data is hidden, ensuring that it can only be manipulated in controlled ways.
- **Interchangeability**: The underlying implementation of the data type can be changed without affecting the code that uses it, as long as the interface remains consistent.
- **Flexibility**: Different implementations of the same interface can coexist. For instance, another stack implementation using arrays could be easily swapped without altering client code.

Here is what an alternative implementation using arrays might look like:

```
module ArrayStack : Stack = struct
```

```
  type 'a t = {
    mutable arr : 'a array;
    mutable top : int;
  }
  exception Empty

  let create () = { arr = [||]; top = 0 }
  let resize stack =
    let new_arr = Array.make (2 * (Array.length stack.arr)) stack.arr.(0) in
    Array.blit stack.arr 0 new_arr 0 stack.top;
    stack.arr <- new_arr

  let push x stack =
    if stack.top >= Array.length stack.arr then resize stack;
    stack.arr.(stack.top) <- x;
    stack.top <- stack.top + 1

  let pop stack =
    if stack.top = 0 then raise Empty;
    stack.top <- stack.top - 1;
    stack.arr.(stack.top)

  let is_empty stack = (stack.top = 0)
end
```

This ArrayStack module adheres to the same Stack signature while internally managing the stack state using an array. Thus, client code using the stack interface does not need to change regardless of whether it uses ListStack or ArrayStack.

ADTs are particularly powerful when coupled with OCaml's extensive type system. Not only can you hide implementations, but you can also create rich, type-safe interfaces that guide correct usage and prevent many classes of errors. This is essential for building complex systems where reliability is paramount.

To conclude, abstract data types in OCaml elevate the modularity and robustness of code by hiding implementation specifics and exposing only the necessary functionality. This principle underpins much of the modular design in OCaml, paving the way for scalable and maintainable software development.

6.4 Functor Basics

In OCaml, a functor is a module that is parameterized by another module. Functors allow developers to create flexible and reusable code by decoupling specific implementations from the functionality provided by a module. This section provides a detailed overview of the basics of functors, their structure, and their usage in OCaml.

A simple functor can be thought of as a function that takes a module as an argument and returns a module as a result. To begin understanding functors, we first need to review some fundamental concepts about modules and their signatures, which have been discussed in previous sections.

To define a functor, we use the functor keyword, followed by the module's parameter, its type, and the resulting module. Consider the following basic example of a functor that creates a module for list operations over any ordered type:

```
module type OrderedType = sig
  type t
  val compare : t -> t -> int
end

module ListOps (M: OrderedType) = struct
  let rec sort lst =
    match lst with
    | [] -> []
    | x :: xs ->
        let small = List.filter (fun y -> M.compare y x < 0) xs in
        let large = List.filter (fun y -> M.compare y x >= 0) xs in
        sort small @ [x] @ sort large
end
```

Here, the OrderedType signature defines an ordered type with a comparable function. The functor ListOps takes a module M conforming to the OrderedType signature and implements a simple list sorting function.

To utilize this functor, we need to provide a concrete implementation of the OrderedType:

```
module Int : OrderedType = struct
  type t = int
  let compare x y = x - y
end

module IntListOps = ListOps(Int)

let sorted_list = IntListOps.sort [3; 1; 4; 1; 5; 9; 2; 6; 5; 3]
```

Defining the module Int and then applying the ListOps functor to this module instantiates ListOps with integer-specific operations. The result is IntListOps, which includes the sort function capable of sorting lists of integers.

Using functors in this way allows significant flexibility. By defining a new module conforming to OrderedType, we can easily instantiate a new instance of ListOps for different types, without rewriting the sorting algorithm. Here is an example with strings:

```
module String : OrderedType = struct
  type t = string
  let compare = String.compare
end

module StringListOps = ListOps(String)

let sorted_string_list = StringListOps.sort ["apple"; "orange"; "banana"; "pear"]
```

In this example, StringListOps now provides a sort function specific to lists of strings. The underlying sorting mechanism remains consistent, while the comparison logic is type-specific.

Functors can also take multiple module arguments if needed. Consider a more complex functor that requires two ordered types to create operations over pairs:

```
module PairOps (M1: OrderedType) (M2: OrderedType) = struct
  type t = M1.t * M2.t

  let compare (x1, y1) (x2, y2) =
    let c = M1.compare x1 y1 in
    if c = 0 then M2.compare x2 y2 else c

  let rec sort lst =
    match lst with
    | [] -> []
    | x :: xs ->
        let small = List.filter (fun y -> compare y x < 0) xs in
        let large = List.filter (fun y -> compare y x >= 0) xs in
        sort small @ [x] @ sort large
end
```

In PairOps, we parameterize the functor by two modules, M1 and M2, both conforming to the OrderedType signature. This functor defines a new type t as a pair of M1.t and M2.t, along with a compare function for these pairs.

We can use this functor to create a module for pairs of integers and strings:

```
module IntStringPairOps = PairOps(Int)(String)

let sorted_pairs = IntStringPairOps.sort [(3, "three"); (1, "one"); (4, "four"); (1, "uno"
    )]
```

By applying PairOps to the previously defined Int and String modules, we create IntStringPairOps, providing a sort function for lists of integer-string pairs.

This section has demonstrated how functors can be used to create parameterized modules, thereby promoting code reuse and maintaining flexible, type-specific operations. By leveraging functors, developers can write more generic and adaptable code, which can be instantiated with different module implementations as needed. Functors enhance modularity and abstraction, central principles in managing large and complex codebases.

6.5 Advanced Functor Usage

In this section, we explore sophisticated techniques for using functors in OCaml, focusing on more advanced patterns and use cases. Functors, which are essentially functions at the module level, enable us to write highly adaptable and reusable code by allowing modules to be parameterized by other modules.

Composing Functors

One advanced technique involves composing multiple functors to build complex module structures. Functor composition refers to the pattern where the output of one functor is used as the input for another.

Consider the following example:

```
module type X = sig
  val x: int
end

module F1 (A : X) = struct
  let fx = A.x + 1
end

module F2 (B : sig
  val fx: int
end) = struct
  let f2 = B.fx * 2
end

module Comp = F2(F1(struct
  let x = 10
end))
```

In this example, F1 is a functor that takes a module of type X and produces a module containing a value incremented by one. F2 is a functor that takes a module containing an integer value and multiplies that value by two. By composing these functors, we construct the final module Comp, which results from first applying F1 to a structure containing the value 10, then applying F2 to the resulting module.

The result is evaluated as follows:

```
Comp.f2;;  (* Result: 22 *)
```

By structuring code in this way, we achieve a high degree of modularity and reuse, allowing independent components to be composed into more complex behaviors.

Recursive Functors

Another pattern involves the use of recursive functors, enabling the definition of data structures that reference themselves in a type-safe manner. However, OCaml does not support directly recursive functors. Instead, we can use a fixed-point combinator approach. Here is an example:

```
module type FunctorialType = sig
  type t
  val value : t
end

module F (Rec : FunctorialType) = struct
  type t = { original: Rec.t; current: string }
  let value = { original = Rec.value; current = "new_value" }
end

module rec Base : FunctorialType = F(Base)
```

In this code sample, we define a module type FunctorialType and a functor F that operates over modules of this type. The module rec construct is used to enable the recursive definition of the Base module, referencing itself within the scope of the functor application.

Parameterized Functors

For some applications, functors need to accept not only modules but also other types of parameters such as integers, strings, or types themselves. OCaml supports this through the use of parameterized modules:

```
module MakePair (A : sig val x : int end) (B : sig val y : int end) = struct
  let pair = (A.x, B.y)
end

module FirstPart = struct
  let x = 5
end

module SecondPart = struct
  let y = 10
end

module Pair = MakePair(FirstPart)(SecondPart)
```

Here, MakePair is a functor that takes two arguments, each of a specific module type with an integer field. It binds the values provided by these modules into a pair. This approach demonstrates the flexibly templated nature of OCaml's functors.

Functor Factories

A powerful application of functors is the creation of functor factories—functors that generate other functors. This model is beneficial when there is a common pattern that needs to be applied but with additional parameters:

```
module MakeAdder (N : sig val n : int end) = struct
  module Add (M : sig val m : int end) = struct
    let sum = N.n + M.m
  end
end

module AdderOf5 = MakeAdder(struct let n = 5 end)

module Result = AdderOf5.Add(struct let m = 3 end)
```

In this example, MakeAdder is a functor that, given a module N with an integer value, produces another functor Add. The inner functor Add then takes another module with an integer value and produces their sum. This entire structure demonstrates how higher-order functors can be constructed for greater flexibility and reuse.

Type-driven Functors

Type-driven functors allow modules to be created based on type properties rather than specific values. This pattern is useful when the behavior of modules depends on specific type characteristics.

```
module type Comparable = sig
  type t
  val compare : t -> t -> int
end

module MakeSet (C : Comparable) = struct
  type element = C.t
  let elements = ref []
  let add x =
    elements :=
      List.sort_uniq C.compare (x :: !elements)
  let mem x = List.mem x !elements
end

module IntCompare = struct
  type t = int
  let compare = compare
end

module IntSet = MakeSet(IntCompare)

IntSet.add 3;;
IntSet.mem 3;; (* Result: true *)
```

In this case, MakeSet is a functor that takes a module conforming to the Comparable signature and produces a set module based on the provided comparison function. This pattern clearly showcases the use of functors driven by type constraints and properties.

By understanding and leveraging these advanced functor usage patterns, one can create more robust, flexible, and maintainable OCaml code. Such patterns promote reusability and abstraction, fundamental principles in large-scale software development.

6.6 Parameterized Modules

Parameterized modules, also known as functors, allow for the creation of modules that take other modules as parameters. This affords a high degree of flexibility and reusability in code design. A parameterized module serves as a function at the module level, where modules are the input and output variables of the function. This section will delve into the precise mechanics of parameterized modules, offering clarity through examples, syntax, common usage patterns, and best practices.

To declare a parameterized module, the module keyword followed by a functor name and parameters is used. Here is a simple example:

```
module MakeStack (Element : sig
  type t
  val compare : t -> t -> int
end) = struct
  type elem = Element.t
  type stack = elem list

  let empty : stack = []

  let push (x : elem) (s : stack) : stack = x :: s

  let pop (s : stack) : stack =
    match s with
    | [] -> failwith "Stack is empty"
    | _ :: rest -> rest

  let top (s : stack) : elem option =
    match s with
    | [] -> None
    | x :: _ -> Some x
end
```

In this example, the parameterized module MakeStack is defined. It expects a module Element that matches the signature specified in the parentheses. The Element module should provide a type t and a function compare.

Practical Examples and Usage

To give a clearer idea of how this is used, consider the following example where we create a specific module for integer stacks:

```
module IntElement = struct
  type t = int
  let compare = compare
end

module IntStack = MakeStack(IntElement)
```

Here we define an IntElement module that satisfies the Element signature expected by MakeStack. We then instantiate a specific module IntStack using the IntElement module.

Using IntStack, all operations we defined in MakeStack become available:

```
let my_stack = IntStack.empty
let my_stack = IntStack.push 42 my_stack
let top_element = IntStack.top my_stack
```

The use of parameterized modules in this way promotes code reusability. The stack implementation is generic and can be used with any type of element as long as it conforms to the given signature. We demonstrate this further by creating a stack of strings:

```
module StringElement = struct
  type t = string
  let compare = compare
end

module StringStack = MakeStack(StringElement)
```

Advanced Usage

Parameterized modules can also take multiple modules as parameters. This allows them to depend on and operate with varying behaviors or constraints dictated by the input modules. Consider a case where we have a module for comparison operations:

```
module type Comparable = sig
  type t
  val compare : t -> t -> int
end

module MakeFineStack (Element : Comparable) (Print : sig
  val print : Element.t -> unit
end) = struct
  type elem = Element.t
  type stack = elem list

  let empty : stack = []
```

```
  let push (x : elem) (s : stack) : stack = x :: s

  let pop (s : stack) : stack =
    match s with
    | [] -> failwith "Stack is empty"
    | _ :: rest -> rest

  let top (s : stack) : elem option =
    match s with
    | [] -> None
    | x :: _ -> Some x

  let print_stack (s : stack) : unit =
    List.iter Print.print s
end
```

In this extended example, MakeFineStack takes two parameter modules: one for defining the element type and comparison function (Element), and another to provide a print function (Print). This further abstracts the stack implementation, allowing it to be used with various element types and custom print functionalities.

Instantiation and Use

When instantiating MakeFineStack, both parameter modules must be provided:

```
module IntElement = struct
  type t = int
  let compare = compare
end

module IntPrint = struct
  let print = Printf.printf "%d\n"
end

module FineIntStack = MakeFineStack(IntElement)(IntPrint)
```

Now FineIntStack can be used to create stacks, perform stack operations, and print the stack elements:

```
let my_stack = FineIntStack.empty
let my_stack = FineIntStack.push 42 my_stack
FineIntStack.print_stack my_stack
```

This produces the following output:

```
42
```

Thus, parameterized modules, or functors, provide a powerful mechanism for module-level abstraction and reuse, essential for building modular and maintainable OCaml code.

6.7 Module Types and Constraints

Modules in OCaml allow for the encapsulation of types, functions, and values, facilitating a more organized and modular code structure. Module types specify the signatures of modules, defining the types of values and functions a module must contain. By using module types, we can enforce certain interfaces, thus providing a layer of abstraction and encapsulation. Constraints further refine these specifications, adding more precise control over the module's implementation.

Module types are declared using the sig and end keywords, encapsulating the types and function signatures within these delimiters. Consider the following example of a module type defining a simple stack abstraction:

```
module type SimpleStack = sig
  type 'a t
  val empty : 'a t
  val push : 'a -> 'a t -> 'a t
  val pop : 'a t -> 'a * 'a t
  val is_empty : 'a t -> bool
end
```

In this module type SimpleStack, we define a polymorphic type 'a t representing the stack, a value empty which is an empty stack, a function push to add an element to the stack, a function pop to remove an element from the stack, and a function is_empty to check if the stack is empty.

To implement a module conforming to this type, we use the : symbol followed by the module type name, ensuring that the module adheres to the specified signature:

```
module SimpleStackImpl : SimpleStack = struct
  type 'a t = 'a list
  let empty = []
  let push x s = x :: s
  let pop = function
    | [] -> failwith "Empty stack"
    | x :: xs -> (x, xs)
  let is_empty s = (s = [])
end
```

The SimpleStackImpl module defines 'a t as a list, uses list operations to implement push, pop, empty, and is_empty, thereby conforming to the SimpleStack signature.

OCaml also allows for adding constraints to module types, refining the general type definitions to more specific ones. Consider a module type with type constraints:

```
module type ConstrainedStack = sig
  type elt
  type t
  val empty : t
  val push : elt -> t -> t
  val pop : t -> elt * t
  val is_empty : t -> bool
end
```

The ConstrainedStack module type specifies a type elt for elements and a type t for the stack. When implementing such a module, we can add constraints to specify the types explicitly:

```
module IntStack : ConstrainedStack with type elt = int = struct
  type elt = int
  type t = elt list
  let empty = []
  let push x s = x :: s
  let pop = function
    | [] -> failwith "Empty stack"
    | x :: xs -> (x, xs)
  let is_empty s = (s = [])
end
```

In IntStack, we constrain elt to be int, making sure the stack works specifically with integers.

Further, using the with construct, we can impose constraints to refine module type definitions. For instance, consider introducing a new module type refined from SimpleStack but constrained for integers:

```
module type IntStackOnly = SimpleStack with type 'a t = int list
```

Here, IntStackOnly refines SimpleStack by constraining the polymorphic stack type 'a t to be an int list.

Implementation in adherence to this refined module type:

```
module IntStackImpl : IntStackOnly = struct
  type 'a t = int list
  let empty = []
  let push x s = x :: s
  let pop = function
    | [] -> failwith "Empty stack"
    | x :: xs -> (x, xs)
  let is_empty s = (s = [])
end
```

This implementation follows the IntStackOnly constraints, ensuring the stack operates with integers.

When dealing with more complex module types, constraints can be applied to enhance the clarity and precision of module definitions. For example, let's define a module type for a binary search tree:

```
module type BST = sig
  type elt
  type t
  val empty : t
  val insert : elt -> t -> t
  val member : elt -> t -> bool
  val delete : elt -> t -> t
end
```

To implement a binary search tree for integer elements:

```
module IntBST : BST with type elt = int = struct
  type elt = int
  type t =
    | Empty
    | Node of {value: elt; left: t; right: t}
  let empty = Empty
  let rec insert x = function
    | Empty -> Node {value = x; left = Empty; right = Empty}
    | Node n -> if x < n.value then Node {n with left = insert x n.left}
              else if x > n.value then Node {n with right = insert x n.right}
              else Node n
  let rec member x = function
    | Empty -> false
    | Node n -> if x = n.value then true
              else if x < n.value then member x n.left
              else member x n.right
  let rec delete x = function
    | Empty -> Empty
    | Node n -> if x < n.value then Node {n with left = delete x n.left}
              else if x > n.value then Node {n with right = delete x n.right}
              else (match n.left, n.right with
                    | Empty, r -> r
                    | l, Empty -> l
                    | l, r ->
                        let rec min_node = function
                          | Empty -> failwith "Unexpected empty tree"
                          | Node t -> if t.left = Empty then t.value else min_node t.left
                        in
                        let min_val = min_node n.right in
                        Node {value = min_val; left = n.left; right = delete min_val n.
                            right})
end
```

This example highlights using constraints to implement an efficient and clear integer binary search tree, adhering to the BST module type's constraints for elt.

Through these example implementations, we recognize the importance of module types and constraints in defining clear, abstract, and enforceable interfaces for OCaml modules. This mechanism enhances code readability, reusability, and maintainability in large-scale software development.

6.8 Nested Modules

OCaml provides a powerful feature for organizing code through the use of nested modules. Nested modules allow developers to encapsulate related functionality within a parent module, promoting better code organization, namespace management, and encapsulation. This section elaborates on the concept of nested modules, their syntax, and practical usage with detailed examples.

Definition and Syntax:

A nested module is a module defined within another module. You can define a nested module using the module keyword inside the body of a parent module. Here is the basic syntax for defining a nested module:

```
module Parent = struct
  module Child = struct
    (* Nested module content *)
  end
end
```

In this example, Child is a nested module inside the Parent module. The Child module has its own scope and can contain types, values, functions, and further nested modules.

Accessing Nested Modules:

To access the contents of a nested module, we use the dot notation. Here is an example demonstrating how to define and access nested module contents:

```
module Parent = struct
  module Child = struct
    let hello () =
      print_endline "Hello from Child module"
  end
end

(* Accessing the function from the nested module *)
Parent.Child.hello ()
```

The function Parent.Child.hello is accessed using the dot notation, which navigates through the module hierarchy.

Practical Usage:

One common use case of nested modules is in separating different but related functionalities. For instance, consider an application dealing with geometrical shapes:

```
module Geometry = struct
```

```
  module Circle = struct
    let pi = 3.14159
    let area radius = pi *. radius *. radius
  end

  module Rectangle = struct
    let area length width = length *. width
  end
end

let circle_area = Geometry.Circle.area 5.0
let rectangle_area = Geometry.Rectangle.area 4.0 6.0
```

In this example, the Geometry module contains two nested modules: Circle and Rectangle, each with its own implementation details.

Encapsulation with Nested Modules:

Nested modules can also be used to hide implementation details. By making certain modules private within a parent module, you can control the visibility of internal details. Consider the following example:

```
module Library = struct
  module Internal = struct
    let secret_function x = x * 2
  end

  let public_function x =
    Internal.secret_function x + 1
end

let result = Library.public_function 3 (* This is allowed *)
let secret = Library.Internal.secret_function 3 (* This will cause an error *)
```

In this case, Internal is a nested module that contains a function secret_function. By not exposing Internal outside the Library module, the implementation details are hidden, promoting encapsulation.

Using Nested Modules in Signatures:

Nested modules can also be part of module signatures, enabling further abstraction and type safety. For example:

```
module type GeometrySig = sig
  module Circle : sig
    val area : float -> float
  end

  module Rectangle : sig
    val area : float -> float -> float
  end
end

module Geometry : GeometrySig = struct
  module Circle = struct
    let area radius = 3.14159 *. radius *. radius
  end
```

```
  module Rectangle = struct
    let area length width = length *. width
  end
end
```

In this example, the signature GeometrySig prescribes that any module matching it must contain nested Circle and Rectangle modules, each with specific type requirements.

Avoiding Naming Conflicts:

Nested modules can help avoid naming conflicts by providing a namespace. For example, consider a scenario where two distinct modules need to use the same function name:

```
module Metrics = struct
  module Length = struct
    let measure () = "Measuring length"
  end

  module Weight = struct
    let measure () = "Measuring weight"
  end
end

let length_measurement = Metrics.Length.measure ()
let weight_measurement = Metrics.Weight.measure ()
```

Here, each nested module has a function measure, but there is no conflict because they belong to different namespaces.

Nested modules increase the modularity and maintainability of code by providing more granular control over organization and encapsulation. These benefits become especially evident in large codebases where logical separation and namespace management are crucial.

6.9 Compilation Units

In OCaml, a compilation unit is the basic building block for structuring code in a modular fashion. Each compilation unit corresponds to a file containing OCaml code, and the filename (without the extension) defines the name of the module represented by that compilation unit. OCaml supports two types of files for compilation units: .ml files, which contain implementation code, and .mli files, which contain interface code.

.ml files contain the actual source code for the module. An example

Foo.ml file might look like the following:

```
(* Foo.ml *)
let add x y = x + y

let multiply x y = x * y
```

To compile this Foo.ml file into a module, you would use the OCaml compiler ocamlc:

```
ocamlc -c Foo.ml
```

This command generates a Foo.cmo file (if you use the bytecode compiler) or a Foo.cmx file (if you use the native code compiler). These files are binary object files that can be linked into an executable or library.

.mli files contain the interface for the module, essentially specifying which parts of the module should be exposed to clients. An .mli file for the previously shown Foo.ml might look like the following:

```
(* Foo.mli *)
val add : int -> int -> int

val multiply : int -> int -> int
```

Compiling the Foo.mli file is similar to compiling the Foo.ml file:

```
ocamlc -c Foo.mli
```

This command generates a Foo.cmi file, which contains the compiled interface. The Foo.cmi file ensures that only the types and values specified in the .mli file are accessible to other modules.

In larger projects, developers commonly organize multiple compilation units by structuring directories correspondingly and generating libraries from these files. The ocamlfind tool facilitates dependency management and linking for complex projects. Assume we have another module that depends on Foo. We might have a file Bar.ml:

```
(* Bar.ml *)
open Foo

let use_addition x y =
  let result = add x y in
  Printf.printf "Result: %d\n" result
```

To compile Bar.ml, assuming Foo.cmo has already been generated:

```
ocamlc -c Foo.cmo Bar.ml
```

Finally, you can link the compiled units into an executable:

```
ocamlc -o my_program Foo.cmo Bar.cmo
```

Executing ./my_program will run the compiled Bar module, which utilizes the Foo module's functionality.

Result: <computed result>

An important aspect of managing compilation units is the use of ocamlbuild, a build automation tool that simplifies the compilation, dependency tracking, and linking stages. With an appropriate _tags file, ocamlbuild can compile and link the entire project efficiently. For instance:

```
ocamlbuild my_program.native
```

When working with more sophisticated projects involving numerous dependencies, OCaml provides tools such as dune for better project management. A dune file specifies the project structure and module dependencies clearly, streamlining the build process without manual intervention.

```
(executable
 (name my_program)
 (libraries foo))
```

With all components in place, executing the build command within the project's root directory initiates compilation and linking according to the dune configuration:

```
dune build
```

In projects integrating multiple modules and third-party libraries, using build systems like dune ensures modular and maintainable code organization, facilitating easier module reuse and dependency management. By adhering to these practices, OCaml developers can efficiently manage compilation units, leading to well-structured, scalable applications.

6.10 Best Practices with Modules and Functors

When working with modules and functors in OCaml, software design principles and coding practices should not be overlooked. This section discusses several best practices that can help you create modular, reusable, and maintainable code.

Designing for Decoupling and Reuse

Effective use of modules involves designing for decoupling and reuse. Keep in mind the Single Responsibility Principle, which states that a module should have only one reason to change. This makes the module easier to understand, test, and reuse. Only include functions and types that are closely related.

```
module type StackSig = sig
  type 'a t
  val empty : 'a t
  val push : 'a -> 'a t -> 'a t
  val pop : 'a t -> ('a * 'a t) option
end

module ListStack : StackSig = struct
  type 'a t = 'a list
  let empty = []
  let push x s = x :: s
  let pop = function
    | [] -> None
    | x :: xs -> Some (x, xs)
end
```

Minimizing Dependencies

Dependencies between modules should be minimized to reduce the complexity of the codebase. Strive to define interfaces or module signatures that expose only what is necessary. Not everything implemented within a module needs to be visible outside of it.

```
module type ComplexSig = sig
  type t
  val create : float -> float -> t
  val add : t -> t -> t
end

module Complex : ComplexSig = struct
  type t = {re: float; im: float}
  let create re im = {re; im}
  let add c1 c2 = {re = c1.re +. c2.re; im = c1.im +. c2.im}
end
```

In the above example, the internal representation of Complex is not exposed outside the module, which allows the implementation to be changed without affecting clients of the module.

Using Functors for Parameterization

Functors enable code reuse by allowing modules to be parameterized over other modules. This can be particularly useful for creating generic data structures or for injecting different behaviors into an algorithm.

```
module type ElemSig = sig
  type t
  val compare : t -> t -> int
end

module MakeSet (Elem: ElemSig) = struct
  type element = Elem.t
  type t = Empty | Node of t * element * t

  let rec add x = function
    | Empty -> Node(Empty, x, Empty)
    | Node(l, v, r) as node ->
        let c = Elem.compare x v in
        if c = 0 then node
        else if c < 0 then Node(add x l, v, r)
        else Node(l, v, add x r)
end
```

Here, the MakeSet functor abstracts over the element type and comparison function, making it versatile for various types that can be compared.

Constraining Functor Parameters

Constraining functor parameters with module types can add robustness and clarity. When a functor takes in a module parameter, it is good practice to specify the expected signature of that module. This adds clarity while ensuring that the provided module complies with the expected interface.

```
module type OrderedSig = sig
  type t
  val compare : t -> t -> int
end

module SetFn (Ord : OrderedSig) = struct
  type elt = Ord.t
  type t = Empty | Node of t * elt * t

  let rec mem x = function
    | Empty -> false
    | Node(l, v, r) ->
        let c = Ord.compare x v in
        c = 0 || (c < 0 && mem x l) || (c > 0 && mem x r)

  let rec add x = function
    | Empty -> Node(Empty, x, Empty)
    | Node(l, v, r) as node ->
        let c = Ord.compare x v in
        if c = 0 then node
        else if c < 0 then Node(add x l, v, r)
        else Node(l, v, add x r)
end
```

In SetFn, Ord is expected to conform to the OrderedSig signature, ensuring that the compare function is available and of the right type.

Avoiding Cyclic Dependencies

Modules should be organized to avoid cyclic dependencies. Cyclic dependencies can lead to complexities that hinder compilation and maintenance. These can be avoided by carefully designing module interfaces and breaking down large modules into smaller, well-defined units.

Documentation and Naming Conventions

Proper documentation and consistent naming conventions are essential. Each module should be accompanied by documentation detailing its purpose, usage, and any constraints. Names should be descriptive to make the code more readable and easier to understand.

Testing Modules and Functors

Test each module and functor individually to ensure they function correctly. Unit tests and property-based tests can help verify the correctness of the implementations. Testing functors can be more complex and may require providing several concrete instances of the parameter modules for thorough verification.

```
(* Test for the ListStack module *)
let test_stack () =
  let stack = ListStack.(push 1 empty |> push 2 |> push 3) in
  match ListStack.pop stack with
  | Some (3, _) -> print_endline "Test passed"
  | _ -> print_endline "Test failed"

test_stack ()
```

```
Test passed
```

This section emphasizes that a disciplined approach to using modules and functors, guided by foundational software design principles, leads to cleaner, more maintainable, and reusable code.

Chapter 7

Error Handling

This chapter focuses on robust error handling in OCaml, beginning with the basics of exceptions and custom exception definitions. It covers the practical use of the Option and Result types for comprehensive error management. Other key topics include error propagation, resource management, and debugging techniques. The chapter also presents best practices for error handling and compares different strategies to help developers write resilient and reliable OCaml programs.

7.1 Introduction to Error Handling

Effective error handling is a critical component of robust software development. In OCaml, error handling can be performed using exceptions and other advanced data structures such as the Option and Result types. Understanding how to handle errors correctly ensures that programs can gracefully manage unexpected situations, maintain integrity, and provide meaningful feedback to users and developers.

Error handling begins with recognizing error conditions. These can be instances where the program encounters an unexpected state or input. For example, dividing by zero, opening a nonexistent file, or receiving invalid input data are typical error conditions that need to be addressed.

OCaml offers multiple mechanisms to handle such errors:

- Exceptions

- The Option type
- The Result type

Exceptions in OCaml follow a conventional paradigm seen in many other programming languages. An error condition raises an exception, which can then be caught and managed or propagated up the call stack. Consider the following basic example using exceptions:

```
let divide x y =
  if y = 0 then
    raise (Failure "Division by zero")
  else
    x / y
```

In this case, if the denominator y is zero, an exception is raised using the Failure exception with an accompanying error message.

Exception: Failure "Division by zero".

The Option type offers a more explicit way to handle the presence or absence of values. Instead of raising exceptions, functions can return an Option type, which can be either Some value or None. Using this approach encourages handling of success and failure cases at every point where an Option value is returned.

```
let safe_divide x y =
  if y = 0 then None else Some (x / y)
```

To use the result of the safe_divide function, one can perform pattern matching to handle both cases:

```
match safe_divide 10 0 with
| None -> print_endline "Division by zero"
| Some result -> print_endline (string_of_int result)
```

The Result type is similar to Option but provides richer error information. The Result type includes constructors Ok for successful results and Error for error cases, allowing the inclusion of an error message or error data.

```
type ('a, 'b) result =
  | Ok of 'a
  | Error of 'b
```

Here's an example using the Result type for safe division:

```
let safe_divide x y =
  if y = 0 then Error "Division by zero" else Ok (x / y)
```

This function will now return a Result type, and pattern matching can again be employed to handle different scenarios:

```
match safe_divide 10 0 with
| Error msg -> print_endline msg
| Ok result -> print_endline (string_of_int result)
```

Handling errors with the Result type provides advantage by making the presence of errors and their potential impact explicit in the type system. This can be particularly beneficial in large codebases where the flow of error states needs to be carefully controlled and communicated.

The choice between using exceptions, Option, or Result types depends on the context of the application and the specific error handling requirements. Exceptions are suitable when errors are rare or when they represent truly exceptional conditions. On the other hand, Option and Result types are preferable when the error conditions are a part of the normal flow of data, as they make error handling explicit and enforce that the errors are managed thoughtfully.

Understanding these basic mechanisms sets the foundation for more advanced error handling strategies discussed in subsequent sections.

7.2 Exception Basics

OCaml provides a flexible mechanism for handling runtime errors through exceptions. Exception handling is an integral aspect of robust programming, allowing developers to manage and respond to unexpected conditions without terminating the program abruptly.

Exceptions in OCaml are similar to those in other languages, such as C++ and Java. They are used to signal error conditions and can be caught and handled by a designated handler. This section delves into the basics of defining, raising, and handling exceptions in OCaml.

Defining Exceptions: In OCaml, exceptions are defined using the exception keyword, followed by an exception name. Optionally, an exception can carry additional data, which is specified similarly to type annotations. Below are examples of simple and parameterized exceptions.

```
exception BasicException
exception ParameterizedException of string
```

BasicException is an exception without additional data, while ParameterizedException takes a string argument, which can be used to pass additional information about the error.

Raising Exceptions: To signal that an error has occurred, the raise function is used. This function takes an exception as its argument. When raise is called, the normal flow of the program is interrupted, and control is transferred to the nearest enclosing exception handler that is equipped to handle the raised exception.

```
let div x y =
  if y = 0 then raise (ParameterizedException "Division by zero")
  else x / y
```

In the example above, the div function raises a ParameterizedException if division by zero is attempted, conveying the error with an informative message.

Handling Exceptions: OCaml provides the try...with construct to handle exceptions. When an exception is raised within the try block, the control flow is transferred to the corresponding with clause, which specifies how to handle the exception.

```
let safe_div x y =
  try
    div x y
  with
  | ParameterizedException msg -> Printf.printf "Error: %s\n" msg; 0
  | _ -> Printf.printf "An unknown error occurred.\n"; 0
```

In the safe_div function, the try...with construct is used to catch exceptions raised by the div function. If a ParameterizedException is caught, a message is printed, and the function returns 0. The wildcard pattern _ is used to catch any other unknown exceptions, ensuring that the function can handle any unexpected error gracefully.

Pattern Matching on Exceptions: Within the with clause, exceptions can be matched using pattern matching, allowing fine-grained control over error handling. This facilitates different actions for different exceptions, improving program reliability and readability.

```
let safe_div_v2 x y =
  try
    div x y
  with
  | ParameterizedException "Division by zero" -> Printf.printf "Cannot divide by zero
      .\n"; 0
  | ParameterizedException msg -> Printf.printf "Other error: %s\n" msg; 0
  | _ -> Printf.printf "An unknown error occurred.\n"; 0
```

The safe_div_v2 function distinguishes between a specific ParameterizedException for division by zero and other instances of ParameterizedException. This exemplifies how pattern matching can enhance error specificity and management.

Exception Propagation: When an exception is not caught in the current scope, it propagates up the call stack. If no suitable handler is found, the exception will propagate to the top level and terminate the program. Proper propagation allows intermediate functions to pass errors up to higher-level handlers, which can then decide the appropriate course of action.

```
let compute_operation x y =
  try safe_div_v2 x y
  with e -> Printf.printf "Handling in compute_operation.\n"; raise e
```

In compute_operation, any exception caught is logged and re-raised, allowing it to propagate further up the call stack.

Overall, understanding these fundamental concepts of exceptions in OCaml empowers developers to write programs that are not only resilient but also maintainable and robust.

7.3 Custom Exceptions

In OCaml, defining custom exceptions is crucial for handling specific error conditions that do not fall under the generic exceptions. Custom exceptions provide better control over error handling, allowing developers to categorize and differentiate between various error types. Moreover, they enhance the readability and maintainability of the code.

Custom exceptions in OCaml are defined using the exception keyword, followed by a name that conventionally starts with a capital letter. Optionally, custom exceptions can carry additional information, such as error messages or data associated with the exception. This feature is particularly useful for debugging and logging purposes.

```
exception MyException
exception AnotherException of string
```

In the example above, MyException is a simple custom exception without any additional information. AnotherException, on the other hand, is a custom exception that carries a string message.

Raising a custom exception is achieved using the raise function, and the syntax mirrors raising built-in exceptions. For instance, raising AnotherException with a specific message is straightforward:

```
raise (AnotherException "This is an error message")
```

Handling these custom exceptions involves pattern matching within the try...with construct. The following example demonstrates how to catch and respond to MyException and AnotherException:

```
try
  (* Some code that might raise a custom exception *)
  raise (AnotherException "A specific issue occurred")
with
| MyException -> Printf.printf "Caught MyException\n"
| AnotherException msg -> Printf.printf "Caught AnotherException with message: %s\
    n" msg
```

Once an exception is caught, the associated action—be it logging the error, providing a fallback solution, or rethrowing the exception—can be conducted accordingly.

Custom exceptions can also be parameterized to carry various types of information. Consider the following example where an exception carries an integer and a string:

```
exception DetailedException of int * string
```

Raising this exception with specific information:

```
raise (DetailedException (404, "Resource not found"))
```

Catching and handling the parameterized exception:

```
try
  raise (DetailedException (404, "Resource not found"))
with
| DetailedException (code, msg) -> Printf.printf "Error %d: %s\n" code msg
```

The above example provides valuable contextual information about the error condition, which can be immensely beneficial for troubleshooting and debugging.

In OCaml programs involving file handling, network communication, or other I/O operations, custom exceptions significantly enhance error management. By defining exceptions that represent specific I/O errors, such as FileNotFound or ConnectionFailed, developers can implement precise error recovery strategies.

Consider a scenario involving file operations. A custom exception can be defined for a file-not-found error:

```
exception FileNotFound of string
```

To simulate file access and raise the custom exception if the file does not exist:

```
let open_file filename =
  if Sys.file_exists filename then
    (* Code to open and process the file *)
    Printf.printf "File %s opened successfully\n" filename
  else
    raise (FileNotFound filename)
```

Handling this exception within the program ensures that the error is captured and managed effectively:

```
try
  open_file "testfile.txt"
with
| FileNotFound filename -> Printf.printf "Error: File %s not found\n" filename
```

In addition to enhancing error management, proper documentation of custom exceptions ensures that other developers or future maintainers of the codebase can understand the purpose and usage of each exception. It is considered best practice to document custom exceptions alongside function signatures and module interfaces.

Custom exceptions also play an essential role when developing libraries or APIs. By providing clear and specific exceptions, users of the library can implement precise error handling mechanisms tailored to their applications.

To encapsulate custom exceptions within a module, the following approach can be taken:

```
module FileOperations = struct
  exception FileNotFound of string

  let open_file filename =
    if Sys.file_exists filename then
      Printf.printf "File %s opened successfully\n" filename
    else
      raise (FileNotFound filename)
end
```

When using the FileOperations module, users can handle the FileNotFound exception as follows:

```
try
  FileOperations.open_file "testfile.txt"
with
| FileOperations.FileNotFound filename -> Printf.printf "Error: File %s not found\n"
    filename
```

This modular approach ensures a clean namespace and avoids potential conflicts with similarly named exceptions in other parts of the program or other modules. The ability to define and manage custom exceptions significantly enhances the robustness and reliability of OCaml programs.

7.4 Using Option Type

In OCaml, the option type is a powerful tool for handling cases where a value might be absent or invalid. It provides an elegant and type-safe way to deal with functions that may fail to return a result or variables that may not hold any meaningful value at a certain point in execution. Understanding and effectively using the option type can significantly enhance the robustness and clarity of your error handling mechanisms.

An option type is defined as follows:

```
type 'a option = None | Some of 'a
```

Here, 'a is a type variable, meaning option can be parameterized with any type. The option type has two constructors: None, which represents the absence of a value, and Some which wraps a value of type 'a.

Consider a function that attempts to find an element in a list:

```
let rec find_opt p = function
  | [] -> None
  | x :: xs -> if p x then Some x else find_opt p xs
```

In this function, find_opt searches for an element in a list that satisfies predicate p. If such an element is found, it is returned wrapped in a Some constructor; otherwise, None is returned to indicate that no matching element exists. This return type clearly communicates that the function may not always produce a valid result.

To handle the option type, pattern matching is commonly used. Consider the following example where we make use of the find_opt function:

```
let print_found_element lst =
  match find_opt ((=) 3) lst with
  | None -> print_endline "Element not found."
  | Some x -> Printf.printf "Element found: %d\n" x
```

In this code, the match expression examines the result of find_opt. If the result is None, it prints "Element not found." If the result is Some x, it unwraps x and prints "Element found: " followed by the value. This approach ensures that all cases are accounted for, thus eliminating potential runtime errors due to missing values.

We can further demonstrate the usability of the option type in a more complex scenario. Suppose we need to safely parse an integer from a string:

```
let int_of_string_opt s =
  try Some (int_of_string s) with
  | Failure _ -> None
```

This function, int_of_string_opt, takes a string s and attempts to convert it to an integer. If the conversion fails (i.e., an exception is raised), it returns None. Otherwise, it wraps the result in Some to indicate success. This technique converts an exception-based mechanism into one that uses the option type, promoting clearer and more manageable error handling.
We can utilize this function as follows:

```
let parse_and_print_int s =
  match int_of_string_opt s with
  | None -> print_endline "Invalid integer."
  | Some i -> Printf.printf "Parsed integer: %d\n" i
```

In this illustration, parse_and_print_int attempts to parse the string and prints either a success message with the parsed integer or an error message indicating that the input was invalid. This use of pattern matching on the option type simplifies handling different scenarios and maintains code readability.

Additionally, OCaml provides utility functions in the Option module to work more conveniently with option types. Some of these functions include map, bind, and get:

```
let option_map_example opt =
  Option.map (Printf.sprintf "Value is: %d") opt
```

In option_map_example, the Option.map function applies a given function (in this case, formatting a string) to the value inside a Some constructor, if it exists, and returns None if the input is None. This functional programming style can make code more concise and expressive.

The option type promotes safer coding practices by making it explicit when a value might be absent. Unlike using null or similar idioms in other languages, the option type forces the programmer to consider both presence and absence cases, leading to more reliable and maintainable code.

7.5 Using Result Type

The Result type in OCaml is a robust alternative to exceptions for handling errors. It allows functions to return a value that signifies either a success or a failure. The Result type is defined as follows:

```
type ('a, 'b) result =
  | Ok of 'a
  | Error of 'b
```

In this type definition, Ok represents a successful computation with a result of type 'a, while Error represents a failure with an error message or code of type 'b. This dual-variant type enables developers to clearly distinguish between successful and failed function results.

To illustrate, let us reconsider a common problem—dividing two numbers—but now using the Result type to handle potential division by zero errors. The function might be implemented as:

```
let divide (numerator : float) (denominator : float) : (float, string) result =
  if denominator = 0.0 then
    Error "Division by zero"
  else
    Ok (numerator /. denominator)
```

This divide function returns Ok with the division result if the denominator is non-zero, or Error with an appropriate error message if the denominator is zero.

To handle the result of such a function, pattern matching is commonly used:

```
match divide 10.0 2.0 with
| Ok result -> Printf.printf "Result: %f\n" result
| Error msg -> Printf.printf "Error: %s\n" msg
```

In this example, the code prints "Result: 5.000000" if the division is successful, and "Error: Division by zero" if an error occurs.

Using the Result type has several advantages over exceptions:

- **Explicit Error Handling:** The type system ensures that the caller of the function handles both success and failure cases explicitly. This reduces the likelihood of unhandled errors.
- **Type Safety:** The compiler enforces the types of results and errors, preventing type mismatches and making the codebase more maintainable.

- **Clearer Flow of Control:** The control flow of the program remains clear and explicit. Pattern matching clearly separates successful paths from error paths, improving code readability.

The Result type is also deeply integrated into many modern OCaml libraries, facilitating error handling in a consistent and structured manner. For example, the Rresult library extends the basic Result type with useful combinators for common operations. Consider the following usecase with chaining operations using bind:

```
open Rresult

let safe_root (x : float) : (float, string) result =
  if x < 0.0 then
    Error "Cannot take the square root of a negative number"
  else
    Ok (sqrt x)

let divide_and_root (num : float) (denom : float) : (float, string) result =
  divide num denom >>= safe_root
```

In this example, divide_and_root first attempts to divide num by denom using the divide function. If successful, the result is passed to safe_-root to compute the square root. The »= operator (bind operator) from Rresult library elegantly chains these operations, propagating errors automatically.

Error handling with Result type can be seamlessly integrated with OCaml's other features. For instance, combinators allow us to map over successful results or apply functions conditionally. Using Rresult library's map function, the safe_root example can be refined as follows:

```
let divide_and_square_root (num : float) (denom : float) : (float, string) result =
  divide num denom |> Rresult.R.map sqrt
```

If divide returns an Ok value, map applies sqrt to the contained value. If divide returns an Error, it is propagated without changes.

For more complex scenarios, error handling strategies using Result type become even more critical. In real-world applications, errors might need logging, wrapping with additional context, or sequence handling. The Rresult library provides functions like reword_error to transform error messages, enhancing the information passed through the error-handling chain:

```
let divide_and_square_root (num : float) (denom : float) : (float, string) result =
  divide num denom
  |> Rresult.R.reword_error (fun msg -> "Divide error: " ^ msg)
  >>= safe_root
```

Here, if the division fails, the error message is prefixed with "Divide error:" before being passed to the next computation step. This added context can greatly improve debugging and user feedback.

Aligning error handling codes with modern OCaml practices by using the Result type not only improves robustness but also emphasizes safety and clarity. With extensive library support and versatile combinators, the Result type structures error handling comprehensively and predictably.

7.6 Error Propagation

Error propagation is a critical aspect of error handling in OCaml that involves the mechanism by which errors are transmitted through various levels of function calls and execution contexts. Effective error propagation ensures that errors are communicated meaningfully to the point where they can be appropriately handled, thereby maintaining program robustness.

In OCaml, errors can be propagated using different methodologies, primarily through exceptions and the use of Option and Result types. Each approach has its benefits and trade-offs, which will be illustrated in this section.

Propagating Errors with Exceptions

When an unexpected situation arises, an exception can be raised to signal an error. Exceptions in OCaml can be propagated up the call stack until they are caught by a corresponding try...with expression. Here is an example illustrating how exceptions are raised and propagated:

```
exception Division_by_zero of string

let safe_divide x y =
  if y = 0 then raise (Division_by_zero "Attempted division by zero")
  else x / y

let division_wrapper x y =
  try
    Printf.printf "Result: %d\n" (safe_divide x y)
  with
  | Division_by_zero msg -> Printf.printf "Error: %s\n" msg
```

Executing division_wrapper 10 0 will output:

```
Error: Attempted division by zero
```

The raise statement in safe_divide propagates the error to division_-

wrapper, where it is caught and handled.

Propagating Errors with Option

The Option type provides a concise and type-safe way to handle potentially absent values. Instead of propagating an exception, functions can return None to indicate failure or Some value to indicate success. Here is an example:

```
let safe_divide x y =
  if y = 0 then None
  else Some (x / y)

let division_wrapper x y =
  match (safe_divide x y) with
  | Some result -> Printf.printf "Result: %d\n" result
  | None -> Printf.printf "Error: Division by zero\n"
```

Executing division_wrapper 10 0 will output:

```
Error: Division by zero
```

Option allows the caller to handle the absence of a value (i.e., an error) explicitly, promoting safer code patterns.

Propagating Errors with Result

The Result type is another powerful mechanism for error handling and propagation, particularly when more sophisticated error reporting is needed. A function using Result can return either Ok value to signify success or Error error to signify failure. Here is an illustrative example:

```
type division_error = Division_by_zero

let safe_divide x y =
  if y = 0 then Error Division_by_zero
  else Ok (x / y)

let division_wrapper x y =
  match (safe_divide x y) with
  | Ok result -> Printf.printf "Result: %d\n" result
  | Error Division_by_zero -> Printf.printf "Error: Division by zero\n"
```

Executing division_wrapper 10 0 will output:

```
Error: Division by zero
```

Using Result provides a clear and type-safe method to handle multiple error kinds, contributing to more maintainable and robust error handling in more complex applications.

Combining Exception Handling with Option **and** Result

Combining different error propagation strategies can be beneficial in complex applications. For instance, exceptions can be used for unexpected situations, while Option and Result can handle common operational errors gracefully:

```
exception Unexpected_error

let safe_divide x y =
  if y = 0 then None
  else Some (x / y)

let enhanced_safe_divide x y =
  match safe_divide x y with
  | Some result -> Ok result
  | None -> Error Division_by_zero

let division_wrapper x y =
  match (enhanced_safe_divide x y) with
  | Ok result -> Printf.printf "Result: %d\n" result
  | Error Division_by_zero -> Printf.printf "Error: Division by zero\n"
  | exception Unexpected_error -> Printf.printf "Unexpected error occurred\n"
```

In the given context, error types are well-defined, explicitly propagated, and properly handled.

By understanding and implementing robust error propagation mechanisms, OCaml developers can create programs that are not only correct and reliable but also capable of gracefully handling a wide variety of error conditions. Effective error propagation directly contributes to the maintainability and readability of code, enabling developers to anticipate and respond to potential failures in their programs.

7.7 Resource Management

In software development, resource management is critical to ensure that your program operates efficiently and correctly. Resources such as file handles, network sockets, and memory allocations must be properly managed to avoid leaks, ensure data integrity, and maintain system stability. Contrary to manual resource management methods found in languages like C, OCaml provides various constructs and patterns to manage resources effectively and safely.

OCaml's garbage collector handles memory management automatically. However, explicit management is required for other system resources. This section explores techniques and best practices for resource management in OCaml, focusing on the usage of the try...with construct, the match statement, and the finally clause.

```
let manage_file filename =
```

```
let file = open_in filename in
try
  (* Process the file *)
  let line = input_line file in
  print_endline line;
  close_in file (* Explicitly closing the file *)
with
| e ->
  close_in file;
  raise e (* Re-raise the exception to propagate it further *)
```

In the above example, the manage_file function reads and prints a line from the given file. Proper resource management is implemented by explicitly closing the file inside both the normal execution flow and the exception handling branch. This ensures that the file handle is released regardless of whether the operation was successful.

Often, multiple resources need to be managed within a single function. Nesting try...with constructs can become cumbersome and error-prone. Instead, the use of combinators or RAII (Resource Acquisition Is Initialization) patterns is recommended. The built-in finally function facilitates this:

```
let finally f cleanup =
  let result =
    try
      f ()
    with e ->
      cleanup ();
      raise e
  in
  cleanup ();
  result
```

The finally function takes two arguments, f for the main operation and cleanup for the cleanup procedure. The main operation is executed within a try block, and if an exception occurs, the cleanup function is invoked before the exception is re-raised. Only after the main operation completes successfully is the cleanup function called again, ensuring complete resource management.

Applying finally to the manage_file example:

```
let with_file filename f =
  let file = open_in filename in
  finally (fun () -> f file) (fun () -> close_in file)
```

Using this combinator pattern, resource management becomes more modular and reusable. The with_file function abstracts the resource initialization and cleanup, allowing you to focus on the core operation.

```
let print_first_line filename =
```

```
with_file filename (fun file ->
  let line = input_line file in
  print_endline line)
```

Now, the print_first_line function simply uses with_file to handle all resource management concerns. This approach simplifies the logic and ensures that file handles are correctly managed.

Another practical approach for resource management involves using higher-level constructs or libraries. The Lwt library, often used for concurrent programming in OCaml, provides a monadic interface that encapsulates resource management within the context of asynchronous operations.

```
open Lwt.Infix

let read_file filename =
  Lwt_io.with_file ~mode:Input filename (fun ic ->
    Lwt_io.read_line ic >>= fun line ->
    Lwt_io.printl line)
```

The Lwt_io.with_file function automatically handles the opening and closing of the file, ensuring that resources are correctly managed even in the presence of asynchronous operations.

In addition to using provided tools, developers should follow certain best practices to ensure robust resource management:

- Always release resources in a finally clause or equivalent to ensure cleanup even in the event of an exception.
- Prefer combinator patterns or higher-level abstractions to reduce boilerplate code and avoid mistakes.
- Leverage libraries that provide built-in resource management support.
- Ensure all resources are initialized and finalized properly within their respective scopes.

Integrating these practices into your development workflow results in resilient and efficient OCaml programs that handle resources effectively, minimizing potential errors and leaks.

7.8 Debugging Techniques

Debugging is an integral component of software development, particularly in a functional language like OCaml, which offers distinctive paradigms and constructs. This section delves into several effective debugging techniques tailored for OCaml programming. Understanding these methods will not only assist in identifying and resolving coding issues but also enhance error handling proficiency, as discussed in previous segments of this chapter.

1. Use of Print Statements

A straightforward yet powerful method to trace program execution and inspect variable values at different stages is using print statements. OCaml provides the print_endline and Printf.printf functions for this purpose.

```
let debug_function x =
  Printf.printf "Input value: %d\n" x;
  let result = x * 2 in
  Printf.printf "Computed result: %d\n" result;
  result
```

While simple, excessive use of print statements may clutter the codebase, making it less readable. Therefore, resort to this technique judiciously or employ conditional print statements that activate only in debug mode.

2. Using the OCaml Debugger

OCaml provides a built-in debugger, ocamldebug, which is instrumental in inspecting the execution flow, setting breakpoints, and evaluating expressions step-by-step. To use ocamldebug, compile the program with debugging symbols:

```
ocamlc -g -o my_program my_program.ml
```

Invoke the debugger with the following command:

```
ocamldebug my_program
```

Within the debugger command line, several commands facilitate debugging:

- break {function_name}: Sets a breakpoint at the beginning of the specified function.
- step: Executes the next program line.

- next: Executes the next line, stepping over function calls.
- print {variable}: Displays the value of the specified variable.
- run: Starts the program execution from the beginning.

Consider the following example, where we set a breakpoint in debug_-function and inspect the value of result:

```
(ocd) break debug_function
(ocd) run
(ocd) next
(ocd) print result
```

The OCaml debugger is highly valuable for understanding runtime behavior and identifying locational errors, especially when managing complex codebases.

3. Logging

For more scalable, maintainable, and controlled debugging, prefer logging over print statements. The Logs library offers structured logging capabilities in OCaml. Install the library using OPAM:

```
opam install logs
```

Incorporate logging into your program as follows:

```
open Logs

let () =
  Logs.set_reporter (Logs_fmt.reporter ())

let debug_function x =
  Logs.debug (fun m -> m "Input value: %d" x);
  let result = x * 2 in
  Logs.debug (fun m -> m "Computed result: %d" result);
  result
```

Using modulation levels like debug, info, warn, and error, logging provides a versatile way to monitor code behavior without stepping through each execution detail manually.

4. Unit Testing with OUnit

Incorporating tests facilitates early bug detection by validating individual components' correctness. The OUnit library is prominent for unit testing in OCaml. To install:

```
opam install ounit
```

Define tests as follows:

```
open OUnit2

let test_function _ =
  assert_equal 4 (debug_function 2);
  assert_equal 10 (debug_function 5)

let suite =
  "TestSuite" >::: [
    "test_function" >:: test_function;
  ]

let () =
  run_test_tt_main suite
```

Execute the tests to ensure function outputs align with expected values, pinpointing abnormalities efficiently.

5. Code Analyzers and Linters

Utilizing code analysis tools helps detect potential errors, style issues, and unoptimized code segments. Merlin is a comprehensive tool providing context-sensitive completion, type information, and linting for OCaml. Install Merlin via OPAM:

```
opam install merlin
```

Integrate Merlin with editors like Vim or Emacs to streamline development workflow, leveraging instant feedback on erratic code segments and improving code quality dynamically.

Integrating debugging techniques such as print statements, logging, unit tests, and code analyzers significantly enhances error detection and resolution capabilities. Each approach facilitates unique aspects of the debugging process, contributing to robust and efficient OCaml programming practices.

7.9 Error Handling Best Practices

Effective error handling is crucial to developing resilient and reliable software. Adopting best practices for error handling will greatly improve the robustness and maintainability of your OCaml programs.

Using Explicit Result Types

One of the foremost best practices is to favor explicit result types, such as option and result, for functions that may fail. By doing so, you can force the caller to handle potential failures at compile time. This explicit approach enhances the readability and predictability of your code base.

```
let find_element lst target =
  let rec aux = function
    | [] -> None
    | x::xs -> if x = target then Some x else aux xs
  in aux lst
;;
```

In this example, rather than raising an exception when the target element is not found, the function returns None, making it clear to the caller that the absence of the element is a possible outcome.

Combining Result Type with Pattern Matching

Pattern matching allows for graceful handling of different outcomes. When working with the result type, which can be Ok of 'a or Error of 'e, pattern matching ensures that all potential branches are covered, promoting exhaustive and robust error handling.

```
type error = Not_found | Invalid_input

let divide x y =
  if y = 0 then Error Invalid_input
  else Ok (x / y)
;;

match divide 10 0 with
| Ok result -> Printf.printf "Result is %d\n" result
| Error Not_found -> Printf.printf "Element not found\n"
| Error Invalid_input -> Printf.printf "Invalid input provided\n"
;;
```

Here, pattern matching is employed to handle both the successful division and the potential error on attempting to divide by zero systematically.

Avoiding Exceptions for Control Flow

Using exceptions for control flow can lead to convoluted code and can mask the underlying logic. Instead, employ exceptions strictly for exceptional states that are not merely alternate flows of usual functionality. Use option and result types for recoverable errors that are expected as part of normal operations.

```
exception Empty_list

let safe_hd = function
  | [] -> None
  | x::_ -> Some x
;;

match safe_hd [1; 2; 3] with
| Some value -> Printf.printf "Head of list: %d\n" value
| None -> Printf.printf "List is empty\n"
```

```
;;
```

Instead of raising an Empty_list exception, the function returns None if the list is empty, making the behavior transparent.

Providing Detailed Error Information

When employing the result type for error handling, the error variant should include detailed information about the failure. This additional context can be invaluable for diagnosing and resolving issues.

```
type error = Division_by_zero | Negative_input of int

let safe_divide x y =
  if y = 0 then Error Division_by_zero
  else if x < 0 || y < 0 then Error (Negative_input (min x y))
  else Ok (x / y)
;;

match safe_divide (-10) 2 with
| Ok result -> Printf.printf "Result is %d\n" result
| Error Division_by_zero -> Printf.printf "Cannot divide by zero\n"
| Error (Negative_input n) -> Printf.printf "Negative input encountered: %d\n" n
;;
```

This function can signal multiple kinds of errors, with the error type conveying specific details, enhancing the capability of downstream error handling.

Leveraging Monad Bindings for Result Types

Utilize monad bindings, such as let-bindings in the result monad, to streamline error-handling code. This approach minimizes boilerplate and makes the code more expressive.

```
let ( let* ) res f = match res with
  | Ok v -> f v
  | Error e -> Error e

let validated_divide x y =
  let* result1 = safe_divide x y in
  let* result2 = safe_divide result1 y in
  Ok result2
;;

match validated_divide 10 2 with
| Ok value -> Printf.printf "Computation succeeded with value: %d\n" value
| Error e -> Printf.printf "Error occurred during computation\n"
;;
```

The let* operator facilitates chaining operations that might fail, reducing boilerplate and harmonizing the handling of both successful and error outcomes.

Integrating these best practices into your codebase will significantly enhance its robustness, making your OCaml applications more reliable and maintainable.

7.10 Comparing Error Handling Strategies

Error handling in OCaml offers multiple strategies, each with unique advantages and disadvantages. Understanding these strategies and their implications is critical in writing resilient and maintainable code. This section delves into comparing different error handling strategies provided by OCaml: exceptions, the Option type, and the Result type. Each approach will be evaluated regarding ease of use, flexibility, readability, and suitability for various scenarios.

Exceptions are a built-in mechanism for handling errors. They allow control flow to be abruptly altered when an error condition is encountered.

```
exception NotFound

let find_element lst elem =
  try
    List.find (fun x -> x = elem) lst
  with
  | Not_found -> raise NotFound
```

In this example, we define a custom exception NotFound and use a try...with block to catch the built-in Not_found exception. If the element is not found, we raise our custom exception. This strategy simplifies handling unexpected conditions by separating error-handling logic from regular code flow.

Another widely-used mechanism is the **Option** type. The Option type represents the possibility of an operation returning either Some result or None.

```
let find_element_opt lst elem =
  try
    Some (List.find (fun x -> x = elem) lst)
  with
  | Not_found -> None
```

In this case, instead of throwing an exception, we return None if the element is not found, otherwise Some value. The caller must handle both possibilities, promoting explicit error handling.

The **Result** type provides a more expressive way to manage errors.

It represents an operation that can either succeed (Ok(value)) or fail (Error(msg)). This allows more expressive error messages and better control over error propagation.

```
type 'a result =
  | Ok of 'a
  | Error of string

let find_element_result lst elem =
  try
    Ok (List.find (fun x -> x = elem) lst)
  with
  | Not_found -> Error "Element not found"
```

Here, we define the result type and return either Ok(value) if the operation is successful or Error("msg") if it fails. This provides additional context about the error, aiding debugging and maintenance.

Evaluating these three strategies, we observe the following:

- **Exceptions** are suitable for handling unexpected errors that should disrupt normal flow and need immediate attention. They simplify code when error handling is not the primary concern of the client code.
- The **Option** type is appropriate for scenarios where the absence of a value is a common and expected result. It enforces the caller to handle the 'none' case explicitly, leading to safer code.
- The **Result** type offers detailed error messages and explicit control flow management for operations that can fail. This is particularly useful in complex systems where understanding the cause of failure is critical.

Choosing the right strategy depends on the specific requirements and context of the application. Using exceptions, while quick, can lead to less predictable control flow and harder-to-debug code. The Option type is excellent for optional values but lacks detailed error information. The Result type balances explicit error handling and informative errors, making it suitable for critical operations where failure is a core concern.

Balancing these strategies by using exceptions for critical or unexpected errors, Option for optional results, and Result for functions with possible failure can lead to robust and maintainable OCaml programs.

Ensure to consistently use and document chosen error handling strategies to maintain code clarity and collaboration efficiency. Through deliberate usage, one can leverage the strengths of each strategy to write resilient and predictable software.

Chapter 8

Input and Output

This chapter examines the mechanisms of input and output in OCaml, starting with basic I/O operations and file handling. It includes detailed discussions on reading and writing files, formatted output, and working with strings. The chapter also covers binary I/O, interaction with the system, handling command line arguments, and networking basics. Additionally, asynchronous I/O techniques are introduced to help manage complex I/O operations effectively.

8.1 Basic Input and Output

Basic input and output operations in OCaml are fundamental to most programs. The OCaml standard library provides modules such as Pervasives (automatically opened in every OCaml program) to facilitate these operations. This section covers the primary functions and methods used for reading from standard input and writing to standard output.

Reading from Standard Input

OCaml provides the read_line function to capture input from the user. This function reads a line of text from the standard input until a newline character is encountered. It returns the input as a string:

```
let user_input = read_line ();;
print_endline ("You entered: " ^ user_input);;
```

In this example, the program waits for the user to enter a line of text and then echoes the input back to the user. The print_endline function is used to ensure that the output is followed by a newline.

For more complex input needs, the OCaml standard library offers several other functions, such as input_line from the Pervasives module to read from channels:

```
let in_channel = open_in "input.txt";;
let line = input_line in_channel;;
print_endline line;;
close_in in_channel;;
```

This code snippet opens a file named input.txt, reads a single line from it, prints the line to standard output, and then closes the file. The open_in and close_in functions manage the file operations, ensuring that resources are properly released.

Writing to Standard Output

To write output to standard output, OCaml's print_string and print_endline functions are commonly used. The print_string function prints a string without a trailing newline, while print_endline includes a newline:

```
print_string "Hello, ";
print_endline "world!";;
```

The above code outputs:

```
Hello, world!
```

If formatted output is required, OCaml's Printf module can be utilized. It provides functions such as printf, eprintf, and sprintf for various output needs. For example:

```
Printf.printf "Name: %s, Age: %d\n" "Alice" 30;;
```

The Printf.printf function formats the string according to the given format specifiers: %s for strings and %d for integers.

OCaml also supports writing to files using the same Printf module. This involves opening a channel and writing to it as shown below:

```
let out_channel = open_out "output.txt";;
Printf.fprintf out_channel "The square of %d is %d\n" 4 (4 * 4);;
close_out out_channel;;
```

This example opens a file named output.txt for writing, writes the specified formatted string to the file, and then closes the file.

Reading and Writing Integers and Floats

In addition to strings, OCaml provides methods for reading and writing integers and floats. For input, the Scanf module is used:

```
let number = Scanf.scanf "%d" (fun x -> x);;
print_endline ("You entered: " ^ string_of_int number);;
```

The Scanf.scanf function reads an integer according to the %d format specifier and then converts it to a string for printing.

For output, both Printf and simple methods like print_int and print_-float can be employed:

```
print_int 42;;
print_newline ();;
print_float 3.1415;;
print_newline ();;
```

These functions print the integer 42 and the float 3.1415 followed by newlines.

Using Channels for I/O

Channels are another significant aspect of OCaml I/O. They are abstract objects representing inputs or outputs, including but not limited to, files, sockets, and more. OCaml provides the in_channel and out_-channel types to work with input and output streams, respectively.

To read from a channel, the input_char function can be used:

```
let in_channel = open_in "input.txt";;
try
  while true do
    let char = input_char in_channel in
    print_char char
  done
with End_of_file ->
  close_in in_channel;;
```

This program reads characters one by one from input.txt until the end of the file, displaying each character.

Similarly, characters can be written to a file using the output_char function:

```
let out_channel = open_out "output.txt";;
output_char out_channel 'A';;
close_out out_channel;;
```

The output_char function writes the character 'A' to output.txt.

End-of-File Handling

Handling the end-of-file (EOF) correctly is crucial for robust I/O operations. The End_of_file exception is raised when the end of a file is reached during input:

```
let in_channel = open_in "input.txt";;
try
  while true do
    let line = input_line in_channel in
    print_endline line
  done
with End_of_file ->
  close_in in_channel;;
```

This pattern ensures that the program reads and prints lines until EOF is encountered, at which point it closes the input channel.

Writing programs that handle input and output correctly and efficiently is essential in OCaml. By understanding and utilizing the provided functions, one can create robust applications that handle a variety of I/O tasks.

8.2 File Handling

File handling in OCaml involves managing the reading from and writing to files, which is essential for data persistence and interaction with external resources. This section provides a comprehensive overview of the file handling capabilities in OCaml, focusing on the core functions and techniques to work with files effectively. We will explore the methods to open, read, write, and close files.

The primary module for file handling in OCaml is the Pervasives module, which is automatically opened, giving direct access to its functions without needing to open the module explicitly. Let's begin by discussing how to open and close files.

Opening and Closing Files

To interact with a file, it must first be opened using the open_in or open_out functions. The function open_in opens a file for reading, while open_out opens a file for writing. Both functions return a file descriptor that can be used for subsequent operations.

```
let input_channel = open_in "input.txt"
let output_channel = open_out "output.txt"
```

After performing the necessary operations on the file, it is crucial to close the file descriptor using the close_in or close_out functions to release system resources.

```
close_in input_channel
close_out output_channel
```

Reading from Files

Reading from files in OCaml can be accomplished using several functions depending on the specific requirements, such as reading line by line or character by character. The input_line function reads an entire line from the input channel:

```
let line = input_line input_channel
```

The input_char function reads a single character:

```
let char = input_char input_channel
```

For more control over how much data to read, the really_input function can read a specified number of bytes into a buffer:

```
let buffer = Bytes.create 8
really_input input_channel buffer 0 8
```

Writing to Files

Writing data to files is facilitated by functions such as output_string and output_char. The output_string function writes a string to the output channel:

```
output_string output_channel "Hello, World!"
```

The output_char function writes a single character:

```
output_char output_channel 'A'
```

For binary data, the output function is useful for writing a specific number of bytes from a buffer:

```
output output_channel buffer 0 8
```

Handling End-of-File

When reading from files, it is crucial to handle the end-of-file (EOF) condition properly to avoid runtime exceptions. This can be done using the input_line function within a loop and catching the End_of_file exception:

```
let rec read_all_lines channel =
  try
    let line = input_line channel in
    print_endline line;
```

```
    read_all_lines channel
  with End_of_file ->
    close_in channel

read_all_lines input_channel
```

Error Handling

Error handling is an essential aspect of file handling since I/O operations are prone to various errors such as file not found, permission issues, and read/write errors. OCaml provides exceptions to manage these errors. For instance, Sys_error can be caught and handled gracefully:

```
try
  let input_channel = open_in "nonexistent.txt" in
  close_in input_channel
with
| Sys_error msg -> Printf.eprintf "Error: %s\n" msg
```

These techniques for file handling in OCaml form the foundation for more complex I/O operations and applications. Properly managing file descriptors, handling errors, and correctly processing data ensure that file interactions are efficient and reliable. These practices are critical for developing robust OCaml programs that interact with the filesystem.

8.3 Reading and Writing Files

Reading and writing files in OCaml involves using the standard library, which provides several modules and functions to facilitate these operations. Key modules include Pervasives, In_channel, and Out_channel. This section explores the different methods of handling files, focusing on how to efficiently read from and write to files using these modules.

To begin with, we look at the basic methods for opening, reading, writing, and closing files.

```
(* Opening a file for reading *)
let input_channel = open_in "input.txt"

(* Opening a file for writing *)
let output_channel = open_out "output.txt"
```

Once a file is opened, data can be read from or written to the file. For reading, we can use functions like input_line, input_char, and input_binary_int. For writing, functions such as output_string, output_char, and output_binary_int are commonly used.

```
(* Reading a line from a file *)
let line = input_line input_channel

(* Reading a character from a file *)
let char = input_char input_channel

(* Writing a string to a file *)
output_string output_channel "Hello, OCaml!"
```

After performing the necessary read or write operations, it is crucial to close the files to release the resources.

```
(* Closing the input channel *)
close_in input_channel

(* Closing the output channel *)
close_out output_channel
```

For more complex file operations, it is essential to handle potential errors, such as trying to read from a non-existent file. OCaml provides exception handling mechanisms using try...with blocks to manage such cases.

```
(* Handling file not found exception *)
let safe_read file =
  try
    let ic = open_in file in
    let first_line = input_line ic in
    close_in ic;
    first_line
  with
  | Sys_error msg -> print_endline ("Cannot open file: " ^ msg); ""
```

In addition to basic plain-text I/O, OCaml also supports binary file operations. To read or write binary data, use functions like input_binary_int and output_binary_int.

```
(* Writing binary data to a file *)
let write_binary file data =
  let oc = open_out_bin file in
  output_binary_int oc data;
  close_out oc

(* Reading binary data from a file *)
let read_binary file =
  let ic = open_in_bin file in
  let data = input_binary_int ic in
  close_in ic;
  data
```

Working with large files often requires reading or writing data in chunks. OCaml's Buffer module is useful for efficiently managing large data during I/O operations.

```
(* Reading a large file in chunks *)
let read_large_file file chunk_size =
  let ic = open_in file in
  let buffer = Buffer.create chunk_size in
  let rec read_chunks () =
    let chunk = really_input_string ic chunk_size in
    Buffer.add_string buffer chunk;
    if String.length chunk < chunk_size then ()
    else read_chunks ()
  in
  read_chunks ();
  close_in ic;
  Buffer.contents buffer
```

For performance-critical applications, handling I/O asynchronously can be beneficial. OCaml's Unix module provides non-blocking I/O operations to manage these efficiently.

```
(* Asynchronous write operation using Unix *)
open Unix

let async_write file data =
  let fd = openfile file [O_WRONLY; O_CREAT] 0o644 in
  let rec write_aux offset =
    let len_written = write fd data offset (String.length data - offset) in
    if len_written > 0 && offset + len_written < String.length data then
      write_aux (offset + len_written)
  in
  write_aux 0;
  close fd
```

This comprehensive approach to file handling in OCaml provides the necessary foundation for efficient and robust I/O operations. Whether dealing with text or binary data, OCaml's standard library offers the tools required to perform these tasks effectively.

8.4 Formatted Output

Formatted output is crucial for producing readable and maintainable display results in OCaml. This section explores the various methodologies and functions available for creating formatted strings and printing them to standard output.

OCaml's standard library provides several methods for formatted output, which can be categorized mainly into three types: printf, fprintf, and sprintf. These functions are analogous to those found in C, with printf outputting to the standard output, fprintf to a specified output channel, and sprintf to a string.

To begin, the Printf module should be opened or referred to explicitly:

```
open Printf
```

printf: This function outputs formatted data to the standard output.

```
printf "Hello, World!\n"
```

The above code outputs:

```
Hello, World!
```

The printf function uses format specifiers that start with the % character. Some common format specifiers include:

- %d – Integer
- %f – Floating-point number
- %s – String
- %c – Character

Consider the following example that demonstrates multiple specifiers:

```
let name = "Alice"
let age = 30
let height = 5.5

printf "Name: %s, Age: %d, Height: %.1f\n" name age height
```

This code produces the output:

```
Name: Alice, Age: 30, Height: 5.5
```

In the format string "Name: %s, Age: %d, Height: %.1f
n", the specifiers %s, %d, and %.1f are used for a string, an integer, and a floating-point number with one decimal place, respectively.

fprintf: Similar to printf, but outputs to a specified output channel. Common output channels include stdout and file channels.

```
let oc = open_out "output.txt"
fprintf oc "Writing to a file: Name: %s, Age: %d, Height: %.1f\n" name age height
close_out oc
```

This example opens a file named output.txt for writing and prints formatted output to it. The file is then closed using close_out.

sprintf: Rather than writing to an output channel, sprintf returns the formatted string.

```
let formatted_string = sprintf "Stored in a string: Name: %s, Age: %d, Height: %.1f"
    name age height
```

In this instance, formatted_string will hold the value "Stored in a string: Name: Alice, Age: 30, Height: 5.5".

kprintf: An advanced function that allows specifying a continuation function to handle the formatted output.

```
let continuation_output str = print_endline ("[Continued] " ^ str)
kprintf continuation_output "Continuation example: %s" "sample"
```

This prints:

```
[Continued] Continuation example: sample
```

Escape sequences are also available for special characters, such as:

- n – Newline
- t – Tab
- " – Double quote
- – Backslash

To handle complex formatting, including padding and alignment, additional flags can be used in format specifiers:

- %-n – Left-justify the result within the given field width n.
- %0n – Pad with zeros instead of spaces.

```
printf "Right-justified: %5d\n" age
printf "Left-justified: %-5d\n" age
printf "Zero-padded: %05d\n" age
```

This produces:

```
Right-justified:    30
Left-justified: 30
Zero-padded: 00030
```

Through these approaches, OCaml's formatted output capabilities allow developers to create structured, clear, and flexible output for various applications, thereby improving the readability and usability of program outputs immensely.

8.5 Working with Strings

Working with strings in OCaml is a fundamental skill that contributes to effective input and output operations. This section explores string manipulation, pattern matching, string conversion, and mutable versus immutable string types. Understanding these concepts is essential for sophisticated input and output processing in OCaml.

Strings in OCaml are sequences of characters. These sequences are immutable, meaning that once a string is created, it cannot be altered. To manipulate strings, new strings must be created. The String module in OCaml's standard library provides numerous functions for these purposes.

String Creation and Basic Operations

Creating strings in OCaml is straightforward:

```
let s = "Hello, OCaml!" ;;
```

The above code initializes a string s with the value "Hello, OCaml!". Strings can be concatenated using the ^ operator:

```
let s1 = "Hello, " ;;
let s2 = "world!" ;;
let s3 = s1 ^ s2 ;; (* s3 has the value "Hello, world!" *)
```

String.length returns the number of characters in a string:

```
let len = String.length s ;; (* len is 13 *)
```

Accessing Substrings and Characters

Extracting substrings or individual characters can be done using specific functions. String.sub extracts a substring from a given string starting at a specified position:

```
let sub_str = String.sub s3 0 5 ;; (* sub_str is "Hello" *)
```

To access individual characters, use String.get:

```
let char = String.get s3 1 ;; (* char is 'e' *)
```

These functions raise the Invalid_argument exception if the position is out of bounds.

Pattern Matching with Strings

OCaml supports pattern matching with strings, which is a powerful feature for conditional processing. Here is an example of pattern matching with strings:

```
let greet s =
  match s with
  | "Hello" -> "Hi!"
  | "Goodbye" -> "Bye!"
  | _ -> "Unrecognized greeting"
;;

let response = greet "Hello" ;; (* response is "Hi!" *)
```

String Conversion

Converting between strings and other data types is a common operation. The string_of_int and int_of_string functions convert between strings and integers:

```
let str_num = string_of_int 123 ;; (* str_num is "123" *)
let int_num = int_of_string "123" ;; (* int_num is 123 *)
```

Similarly for floating-point numbers, string_of_float and float_of_-string are used:

```
let str_float = string_of_float 3.14 ;; (* str_float is "3.14" *)
let float_num = float_of_string "3.14" ;; (* float_num is 3.14 *)
```

Mutable Strings with Bytes Module

Although standard strings in OCaml are immutable, mutable strings can be managed using the Bytes module. The Bytes module allows the creation and manipulation of mutable sequences of characters. Here is how to create and modify a mutable string:

```
let b = Bytes.of_string "Hello" ;;
Bytes.set b 0 'J' ;;
let mutable_str = Bytes.to_string b ;; (* mutable_str is "Jello" *)
```

Bytes.of_string converts an immutable string to a mutable bytes type, and Bytes.to_string converts it back to an immutable string. Intermediate operations such as Bytes.set can modify the individual characters.

Advanced String Manipulation

Advanced string manipulation techniques include using regular expressions, which require the Str module. The following example demonstrates how to use regular expressions in OCaml:

```
#load "str.cma" ;; (* Ensure Str module is loaded *)

let regex = Str.regexp "world" ;;
let result = Str.replace_first regex "OCaml" s3 ;; (* result is "Hello, OCaml!" *)
```

The code above replaces the first occurrence of the pattern "world" in the string s3 with "OCaml".

String manipulation is integral to handling input and output effectively. With these foundational concepts and functions at your disposal, you can perform complex string operations, enabling efficient data processing, and user interaction in OCaml applications.

8.6 Binary I/O

Handling binary input and output (I/O) in OCaml allows for the efficient reading and writing of data in its raw format. This enables applications to work with data structures more directly and can lead to enhanced performance. In situations where exact fidelity of data storage and retrieval is crucial, such as in database applications, file compression programs, or network communication, binary I/O serves as a crucial tool.

open and output channels in OCaml can be used for reading from and writing to binary files. These channels facilitate the handling of binary data, providing functions to read and write data in various formats (bytes, integers, floating-point numbers, etc.) without the need for conversion to and from textual representation.

```
let read_binary_file filename =
  let ic = open_in_bin filename in
  let n = in_channel_length ic in
  let data = Bytes.create n in
  really_input ic data 0 n;
  close_in ic;
  data
```

In the above code, open_in_bin opens the file named filename in binary mode. The in_channel_length function determines the file's length, and Bytes.create allocates a mutable byte sequence to hold the file's contents. The really_input function reads n bytes from the input channel ic into data, starting at position 0. Finally, the close_in function closes the input channel.

For writing binary data to a file, the following pattern can be used:

```
let write_binary_file filename data =
  let oc = open_out_bin filename in
  output_bytes oc data;
  close_out oc
```

Here, open_out_bin opens the file filename in binary mode for writing, and output_bytes writes the contents of the data byte sequence to the output channel oc. The function close_out then closes the output channel.

When dealing with structured data, converting data to and from raw bytes manually can be error-prone and cumbersome. It's more optimal to use a data serialization library such as Marshal or external binary protocols like Protocol Buffers.

Using the Marshal module, you can easily serialize and deserialize arbitrary OCaml data structures:

```
let serialize_to_file filename data =
  let oc = open_out_bin filename in
  Marshal.to_channel oc data [];
  close_out oc

let deserialize_from_file filename =
  let ic = open_in_bin filename in
  let data = Marshal.from_channel ic in
  close_in ic;
  data
```

The Marshal.to_channel function converts the data into a binary representation and writes it to the output channel oc. The Marshal.from_channel function reads the binary data from the input channel ic and reconstructs the original data structure.

For more complex I/O tasks where higher-level abstractions are useful, leveraging libraries designed for additional functionalities might be beneficial. For instance, working with networking or asynchronous I/O benefits from using libraries like Lwt or Async, which introduce abstractions for managing concurrency and non-blocking operations.

Binary I/O operations are precise and efficient, yet they require careful handling of data structures and attention to detail regarding byte ordering, data alignment, and endianness. Properly handling these considerations ensures that the data read from a binary file or received from a network socket is accurately interpreted.

Combining binary I/O techniques with robust libraries and OCaml's type-safe features allows for highly efficient and reliable processing of data in its raw form, optimizing both performance and storage.

8.7 Interacting with the System

Interacting with the underlying system is a crucial capability for many applications. In OCaml, system interactions can be performed using the Unix module, which provides various functionalities for interfacing with the operating system. This section covers some essential operations such as executing commands, working with environment variables, and handling signals.

To access the Unix module, ensure that your file includes the following line:

```
open Unix
```

Executing System Commands

The Unix module provides several functions to execute system commands. One of the primary functions is system, which is defined as follows:

```
val system : string -> process_status
```

The system function takes a command string as an argument and executes it in a subshell. The execution result is returned as a process_status type, which can be either WEXITED, WSIGNALED, or WSTOPPED, representing the exit status, signal termination, or stop signal respectively. Example usage:

```
let () =
  match Unix.system "ls -l" with
  | Unix.WEXITED code -> Printf.printf "Exited with code %d\n" code
  | Unix.WSIGNALED signal -> Printf.printf "Killed by signal %d\n" signal
  | Unix.WSTOPPED signal -> Printf.printf "Stopped by signal %d\n" signal
```

The above example runs the ls -l command and prints the result based on the process_status.

Working with Environment Variables

Environment variables store useful configuration information. You can retrieve and manipulate these variables using functions like getenv and putenv.

To retrieve the value of an environment variable:

```
let path = Unix.getenv "PATH"
```

If the variable does not exist, Unix.getenv raises an exception. To avoid this, check if the variable is defined:

```
let get_env_var var =
  try Some (Unix.getenv var) with
  | Not_found -> None
```

To set or modify an environment variable, use putenv:

```
Unix.putenv "PATH" "/usr/local/bin:/usr/bin:/bin"
```

Handling Signals

Signal handling is essential for writing robust applications. The Unix module offers functions to handle signals such as sigint, sigterm, etc.

Define a signal handler as follows:

```
let signal_handler signal =
  Printf.printf "Received signal %d\n" signal;
  exit 0
```

To associate the handler with a signal (e.g., sigint):

```
let () =
  Sys.set_signal Sys.sigint (Sys.Signal_handle signal_handler)
```

In this example, pressing Ctrl+C (sends sigint) will trigger the signal_-handler.

Creating and Managing Processes

The create_process function is another powerful way to start new processes. It allows you to specify the executable, its arguments, environment, and redirections for stdin, stdout, and stderr.

The function definition is:

```
val create_process :
  string -> string array -> file_descr -> file_descr -> file_descr -> int
```

Here is an example that creates a process for the ls command:

```
let () =
  let pid = Unix.create_process "ls" [| "ls"; "-l" |] Unix.stdin Unix.stdout Unix.stderr
      in
  ignore (Unix.waitpid [] pid)
```

The Unix.create_process function returns the child process ID, and the Unix.waitpid function waits for the process to terminate.

Working with Pipes

Pipes enable inter-process communication. Use pipe to create a pipe, which returns a pair of file descriptors (one for reading, one for writing).

Example of creating a child process to communicate via a pipe:

```
let () =
  let (read_fd, write_fd) = Unix.pipe () in
  match Unix.fork () with
  | 0 ->
    Unix.close read_fd;
    Unix.dup2 write_fd Unix.stdout;
    Unix.execvp "ls" [| "ls"; "-l" |]
  | pid ->
    Unix.close write_fd;
    let buffer = Bytes.create 1024 in
    let n = Unix.read read_fd buffer 0 1024 in
    Printf.printf "Output: %s" (Bytes.sub_string buffer 0 n);
    Unix.close read_fd;
    ignore (Unix.waitpid [] pid)
```

This example showcases how a parent process creates a pipe and a child process writes the output of ls -l to the pipe, while the parent reads and prints it.

Understanding these system interaction techniques enriches your ability to write versatile and robust OCaml applications by efficiently leveraging underlying system resources and capabilities.

8.8 Handling Command Line Arguments

When developing OCaml programs, it is frequently necessary to interact with the command line to retrieve arguments supplied by the user at runtime. Command line arguments can be used to alter the behavior of your program, supply necessary input parameters, and configure various options.

OCaml provides a straightforward mechanism for handling command line arguments via the Sys.argv array. The Sys.argv array is an array of strings where the first element is the name of the executable program, and the subsequent elements are the arguments passed to the program.

To illustrate, consider the following simple example where we print all command line arguments provided to the program:

```
(* file: print_args.ml *)
let () =
  let n = Array.length Sys.argv in
  for i = 0 to n - 1 do
    Printf.printf "Argument %d: %s\n" i Sys.argv.(i)
  done
```

In this code, Array.length Sys.argv is used to obtain the number of command line arguments, and a for loop iterates through each argument, printing its index and value.

Example Execution

Assuming the above code is compiled to produce an executable named print_args, here is an example execution with command line parameters:

```
$ ./print_args first_argument second_argument
Argument 0: ./print_args
Argument 1: first_argument
Argument 2: second_argument
```

Parsing Command Line Arguments

For more complex handling of command line arguments, OCaml provides the Arg module from the standard library. The Arg module simplifies the process of defining and parsing command line options using various combinators.

A common approach involves defining a list of possible command line options and associating each option with an action or variable that stores the result. Here's a simple example demonstrating the usage of the Arg module:

```
(* file: parse_args.ml *)
let input_file = ref ""
let verbose = ref false

let speclist = [
  ("-i", Arg.Set_string input_file, "Input file");
  ("-v", Arg.Set verbose, "Enable verbose mode")
]

let usage_msg = "Usage: parse_args [options]"
let () = Arg.parse speclist print_endline usage_msg

let () =
  Printf.printf "Input file: %s\n" !input_file;
  Printf.printf "Verbose mode: %b\n" !verbose
```

In this example, we define two references, input_file and verbose, to store the values associated with the -i and -v options. The speclist contains tuples that describe each command line option, the associated action, and a string describing the option.

The function Arg.parse parses the command line arguments according to the options specified in speclist. Remaining arguments (those that do not match any specified options) are passed to the function provided as the second argument to Arg.parse; in this case, print_endline. The third argument is a description of usage displayed if inappropriate arguments are supplied.

Example Execution with Parsing

Consider the execution of the above program with the following command line parameters:

```
$ ./parse_args -i input.txt -v some_unrecognized_argument
some_unrecognized_argument
Input file: input.txt
Verbose mode: true
```

The output shows that the -i option correctly sets the input_file reference, and the -v flag enables verbose mode. The unrecognized argument, some_unrecognized_argument, is passed to print_endline.

Advanced Argument Handling

To handle more advanced scenarios, the Arg module allows for custom actions. One can define functions that will be called when their associated options are encountered. This is useful when the action requires more than simply setting a variable or printing a value.

Consider a scenario where we might want to check the validity of an input file before proceeding:

```
(* file: advanced_args.ml *)
let input_file = ref ""
let set_input_file filename =
  if Sys.file_exists filename then
    input_file := filename
  else
    raise (Arg.Bad ("File not found: " ^ filename))

let verbose = ref false
let speclist = [
  ("-i", Arg.String set_input_file, "Input file");
  ("-v", Arg.Set verbose, "Enable verbose mode")
]

let usage_msg = "Usage: advanced_args [options]"
let () = Arg.parse speclist print_endline usage_msg

let () =
  Printf.printf "Input file: %s\n" !input_file;
  Printf.printf "Verbose mode: %b\n" !verbose
```

Safety Considerations

When working with command line arguments, it is crucial to handle potential errors gracefully. Use the Arg.Bad exception to inform users about incorrect or missing arguments. Additionally, take care to verify the validity and security of input files or other sensitive parameters to protect against malicious input.

This detailed examination of handling command line arguments in OCaml equips you with the knowledge to create flexible and user-friendly applications that respond dynamically to user input provided via the command line.

8.9 Networking Basics

Networking in OCaml provides a powerful means to build distributed applications, interact with remote servers, and transmit data over networks. To effectively utilize networking capabilities in OCaml, we leverage the 'Unix' module, which enables socket programming. We will explore essential concepts, including socket creation, binding, listening, accepting connections, and communicating through sockets.

Sockets are potent abstractions for network communication that encapsulate endpoints in communication channels. They can be used for various protocols, with the most common being TCP (Transmission Control Protocol) and UDP (User Datagram Protocol). TCP is connection-oriented and provides reliable, ordered, and error-checked delivery of a stream of bytes. In contrast, UDP is connectionless and suitable for applications where speed is crucial, and occasional data loss is acceptable.

To create a socket in OCaml for TCP communication, we use the socket function from the 'Unix' module. The socket function requires three parameters: the address domain, the socket type, and the protocol. The address domain specifies the communication domain (e.g., 'Unix.PF_INET' for IPv4 addresses). The socket type indicates whether the socket is stream-based (e.g., 'Unix.SOCK_STREAM' for TCP) or datagram-based (e.g., 'Unix.SOCK_DGRAM' for UDP). The protocol is usually set to 0, letting the system select the appropriate protocol based on the previous parameters.

```
let tcp_socket = Unix.socket Unix.PF_INET Unix.SOCK_STREAM 0
```

After creating a socket, the next step is to bind it to a specific address and port. Binding a socket associates it with a local endpoint, making it ready to accept incoming connections on that address and port. To bind a socket, we use the bind function. The address is represented by the sockaddr type. For an IPv4 address, we use the ADDR_INET constructor:

```
let address = Unix.ADDR_INET (Unix.inet_addr_any, 8080)
```

```
let () = Unix.bind tcp_socket address
```

With the socket bound, we configure it to listen for incoming connection requests. The listen function is used to mark the socket as a passive socket, one that will be used to accept incoming connection requests. The listen function also takes an integer parameter specifying the backlog, which is the maximum number of pending connections that can be queued:

```
let backlog = 10
let () = Unix.listen tcp_socket backlog
```

Once the socket is in a listening state, it can accept incoming connections using the accept function. This function blocks until a connection attempt is made, then returns a new socket descriptor for the established connection and the address of the connecting peer:

```
let (client_socket, client_address) = Unix.accept tcp_socket
```

With a connection established, communication can occur over the client socket. Data can be sent and received using the send and recv functions or the higher-level Unix.write and Unix.read functions:

```
let message = "Hello, client!"
let bytes_sent = Unix.send client_socket message 0 (String.length message) []
let buffer = Bytes.create 1024
let bytes_received = Unix.recv client_socket buffer 0 1024 []
let received_message = Bytes.sub_string buffer 0 bytes_received
```

The above code snippet demonstrates sending a message to the client and receiving a message from the client. The send function transmits data over a socket, and the recv function reads data from the socket into a buffer of type Bytes.t.

For client-side socket programming, the process involves creating a socket, connecting to a remote server, and then communicating through the socket. The connect function establishes a connection to the server:

```
let server_address = Unix.ADDR_INET (Unix.inet_addr_of_string "127.0.0.1", 8080)
let () = Unix.connect tcp_socket server_address
```

With the connection established, the client can communicate with the server in a similar manner as shown in the server-side communication example. After communication is complete, closing the socket is crucial to free up system resources. The close function performs this operation:

```
let () = Unix.close tcp_socket
```

By understanding these fundamental operations, you can build more complex networking applications in OCaml. The 'Unix' module provides a broad range of functions to accommodate various networking needs, enabling efficient and reliable communication between distributed systems.

8.10 Asynchronous I/O

Asynchronous I/O refers to the ability of a program to initiate I/O operations and continue processing other tasks before the I/O operation completes. This non-blocking approach is particularly useful for applications that require high levels of responsiveness or need to handle multiple I/O operations concurrently.

In OCaml, asynchronous I/O can be achieved using libraries such as Lwt (Lightweight Threads) and Async. These libraries provide abstractions for managing asynchronous operations, significantly simplifying the process compared to manual event loop management.

Lwt is one of the most widely used libraries for asynchronous programming in OCaml. It allows you to write concurrent code in a straightforward manner using promises and cooperative threading.

To include Lwt in your project, you need to install the package and load it in your OCaml environment. Assuming you are using opam, OCaml's package manager, the installation command is as follows:

```
opam install lwt
```

After installing Lwt, you can open the library in your OCaml file:

```
open Lwt
```

Next, let's examine a simple example where we read from a file asynchronously using Lwt.

```
(* Import Lwt and Lwt_io modules *)
open Lwt
open Lwt_io

(* Define an asynchronous function to read from a file *)
let read_file_async filename =
  Lwt_io.with_file ~mode:Input filename
    (fun file ->
      Lwt_io.read file >>= fun content ->
      Lwt.return content)

(* Execute the asynchronous I/O and print the result *)
```

```
let () =
  let filename = "example.txt" in
  let read_content = Lwt_main.run (read_file_async filename) in
  print_endline read_content
```

In this example: - open Lwt and open Lwt_io include the necessary modules. - read_file_async is defined as an asynchronous function that reads the contents of the specified file. - The Lwt_io.with_file function is used to open the file in input mode (mode:Input). - The file content is read using Lwt_io.read. - Lwt.return is used to encapsulate the content in a promise. - Lwt_main.run is called to execute the asynchronous operation and obtain the result synchronously for printing.

To understand how asynchronous operations can be sequenced, consider the following extended example where multiple files are read concurrently:

```
(* Define an asynchronous function to read multiple files *)
let read_files_async filenames =
  let read_single_file filename =
    Lwt_io.with_file ~mode:Input filename Lwt_io.read
  in
  Lwt_list.map_p read_single_file filenames

(* Execute the asynchronous I/O and process the results *)
let () =
  let filenames = ["file1.txt"; "file2.txt"; "file3.txt"] in
  let file_contents = Lwt_main.run (read_files_async filenames) in
  List.iter print_endline file_contents
```

In this example: - read_single_file is a helper function to read a single file asynchronously. - read_files_async reads multiple files concurrently using Lwt_list.map_p, which applies the async function read_single_file to each filename in the list. - Lwt_main.run executes the asynchronous read operation, returning a list of file contents. - List.iter print_endline prints each file's content.

Asynchronous I/O is particularly advantageous in network programming. The following example demonstrates how Lwt can be used for asynchronous socket communication:

```
open Lwt
open Lwt_io

let handle_client client_socket =
  let%lwt input_channel = of_fd ~mode:Input client_socket in
  let%lwt output_channel = of_fd ~mode:Output client_socket in
  let%lwt message = read_line input_channel in
  let%lwt () = write_line output_channel (String.uppercase_ascii message) in
  Lwt.return_unit

let start_server () =
  let socket_address = Unix.ADDR_INET (Unix.inet_addr_loopback, 8080) in
```

```
  let%lwt server_socket = Lwt_unix.(socket PF_INET SOCK_STREAM 0) in
  let%lwt () = Lwt_unix.bind server_socket socket_address in
  let%lwt () = Lwt_unix.listen server_socket 10 in
  let rec accept_connections () =
    let%lwt client_socket, _ = Lwt_unix.accept server_socket in
    let%lwt () = handle_client client_socket in
    accept_connections ()
  in accept_connections ()

let () = Lwt_main.run (start_server ())
```

In this example: - handle_client handles communication with a connected client, reading a line, processing it, and sending a response. - start_server initializes and starts a server socket listening on port 8080. - The server socket is created using Lwt_unix.socket and bound to the local address and port using Lwt_unix.bind. - Lwt_unix.listen is used to mark the socket as a passive socket ready to accept incoming connections. - accept_connections endlessly accepts new client connections and spawns the handle_client function for each.

By utilizing the capabilities of Lwt, OCaml allows you to manage asynchronous I/O straightforwardly, promoting efficient and responsive application design.

Chapter 9

Concurrency and Parallelism

This chapter explores concurrency and parallelism in OCaml, beginning with an introduction to their foundational concepts. It covers concurrency with threads, parallelism with Multicore OCaml, and the use of promises and futures. Topics include message passing, shared state and synchronization, and asynchronous programming. The chapter also addresses task scheduling, key concurrency patterns, and techniques for debugging concurrent programs, equipping readers with the tools to write efficient and reliable concurrent applications.

9.1 Introduction to Concurrency and Parallelism

In the domain of computer science, concurrency and parallelism are core concepts that provide the framework for efficient and effective execution of tasks. These concepts not only improve the performance of programs but also enable the development of complex and responsive applications.

Concurrency refers to the ability of a system to handle multiple tasks at the same time. In this context, tasks do not necessarily run simultaneously; rather, they may be executed in an interleaved fashion. Concurrency is utilized to improve the responsiveness of applications, especially in scenarios where tasks have varying execution times or require waiting for external events, such as I/O operations.

Parallelism, on the other hand, involves the simultaneous execution of multiple tasks. Parallelism leverages multiple processing units (e.g., cores or processors) to maximum advantage, reducing the overall runtime of computationally intensive tasks. Parallelism is a subset of concurrency and can be considered as a means of achieving concurrency through the distribution of tasks across multiple processing units.

Understanding the distinctions and interplay between concurrency and parallelism is crucial for developing high-performance OCaml programs. In this section, we will explore how these concepts are implemented in OCaml, providing the foundation necessary to build efficient concurrent and parallel applications.

Concept of Threads:

In OCaml, concurrency is typically achieved using threads. A thread is a unit of execution within a process. In a multi-threaded OCaml program, multiple threads run concurrently within the same address space, sharing resources such as memory.

Here is an example of creating and managing threads using the Thread module in OCaml:

```
open Thread

(* Function to be executed by the thread *)
let thread_function () =
  print_endline "Thread has started execution.";
  Unix.sleep 2;
  print_endline "Thread has finished execution."

(* Creating a new thread *)
let my_thread = Thread.create thread_function ()

(* Main thread continues execution *)
let () =
  print_endline "Main thread is running.";
  Thread.join my_thread;
  print_endline "Main thread is done.";
```

This example creates a new thread that executes thread_function. The main thread continues to run concurrently, and then waits for the created thread to finish using Thread.join.

Concept of Parallelism:

With the advent of multicore processors, OCaml has introduced Multicore OCaml to facilitate parallelism. Multicore OCaml extends the standard OCaml runtime to support parallel execution on multiple cores.

Here is an example of utilizing parallelism in OCaml:

```
open Domainslib

let pool = Task.setup_pool ~num_domains:4

let fib n =
  let rec aux n =
    if n <= 1 then n
    else aux (n - 1) + aux (n - 2)
  in
  aux n

let parallel_fib n =
  Task.run pool (fun _ ->
    Task.parallel_for pool ~start:0 ~finish:(n-1)
      ~body:(fun i -> fib (i mod 10)))

let () =
  let result = parallel_fib 20 in
  print_endline ("Result: " ^ string_of_int result);
  Task.teardown_pool pool
```

In this example, we utilize the Domainslib library to set up a pool of domains (lightweight, parallel execution contexts). We then use Task.parallel_for to distribute the computation of Fibonacci numbers in parallel across the domains.

Synchronization:

Concurrency and parallelism in OCaml often require synchronization mechanisms to coordinate the execution of threads and to prevent data races. Common synchronization primitives include mutexes, condition variables, and atomic operations.

The following is an example of using a mutex for synchronization:

```
open Thread
open Mutex

let mutex = Mutex.create ()
let counter = ref 0

let increment_counter () =
  Mutex.lock mutex;
  counter := !counter + 1;
  Mutex.unlock mutex

let parallel_increment n =
  let threads = Array.init n (fun _ -> create increment_counter ()) in
  Array.iter join threads

let () =
  parallel_increment 10;
  print_endline ("Counter: " ^ string_of_int !counter)
```

In this example, a mutex is used to protect access to the shared variable counter. Threads increment the counter in a safe manner by locking the mutex before the increment operation and unlocking it afterward.

Understanding these foundational concepts of concurrency and parallelism positions us to delve deeper into their application using advanced techniques and tools provided by OCaml. This knowledge enhances our ability to design and manage concurrent tasks effectively, leveraging the full potential of modern multicore processors.

9.2 Concurrency with Threads

Thread-based concurrency in OCaml involves the utilization of multiple threads within a single process to perform tasks concurrently. This leverages the Thread module in OCaml's standard library, facilitating the spawning, management, and synchronization of threads. Threads share the same memory space, allowing easy communication but also necessitating careful synchronization to avoid race conditions.

To begin working with threads, it is essential to understand the basic operations: creating and starting threads, using mutexes for synchronization, and handling shared data structures.

Creating and Starting Threads

Thread creation in OCaml is straightforward, using the Thread.create function which takes a function and an argument for the function. The new thread executes the provided function.

```
let thread_function n =
  Printf.printf "Thread %d is running\n" n

let _ =
  let t1 = Thread.create thread_function 1 in
  let t2 = Thread.create thread_function 2 in
  Thread.join t1;
  Thread.join t2
```

In this example, thread_function prints a message indicating the thread number. Two threads are created, t1 and t2, passing different arguments to the same function. The Thread.join function waits for the threads to finish.

```
Thread 1 is running
Thread 2 is running
```

Synchronization with Mutexes

When multiple threads access shared resources, synchronization mechanisms such as mutexes are required to avoid race conditions. The Mutex module provides the tools for this.

```
let counter = ref 0
let mutex = Mutex.create ()

let thread_increment () =
  for _ = 1 to 1000 do
    Mutex.lock mutex;
    incr counter;
    Mutex.unlock mutex;
  done

let _ =
  let t1 = Thread.create thread_increment () in
  let t2 = Thread.create thread_increment () in
  Thread.join t1;
  Thread.join t2;
  Printf.printf "Counter value: %d\n" !counter
```

Here, counter is shared among threads, and mutex ensures exclusive access. Each thread increments the counter 1000 times, and the final value is printed.

```
Counter value: 2000
```

The use of Mutex.lock before accessing counter and Mutex.unlock afterward ensures that one thread at a time modifies the shared resource.

Handling Shared Data Structures

For complex data structures, using mutexes to protect each operation is crucial. Consider a shared queue where multiple threads might enqueue and dequeue items.

```
module SafeQueue = struct
  type 'a t = {
    queue: 'a Queue.t;
    mutex: Mutex.t;
  }

  let create () = {
    queue = Queue.create ();
    mutex = Mutex.create ();
  }

  let enqueue q x =
    Mutex.lock q.mutex;
    Queue.add x q.queue;
    Mutex.unlock q.mutex
```

```
  let dequeue q =
    Mutex.lock q.mutex;
    try
      let x = Queue.take q.queue in
      Mutex.unlock q.mutex;
      Some x
    with Queue.Empty ->
      Mutex.unlock q.mutex;
      None
end

let queue = SafeQueue.create ()

let thread_enqueue n =
  for i = 1 to 5 do
    SafeQueue.enqueue queue (n, i);
    Thread.delay 0.1;
  done

let thread_dequeue () =
  for _ = 1 to 5 do
    match SafeQueue.dequeue queue with
    | Some (n, i) -> Printf.printf "Dequeued from thread %d: %d\n" n i
    | None -> ()
  done

let _ =
  let t1 = Thread.create thread_enqueue 1 in
  let t2 = Thread.create thread_enqueue 2 in
  let t3 = Thread.create thread_dequeue () in
  Thread.join t1;
  Thread.join t2;
  Thread.join t3
```

This module defines a thread-safe queue. Both enqueue and dequeue functions lock the mutex before modifying the queue, ensuring safe concurrent access. Two threads enqueue items, and one dequeues them, displaying the results.

```
Dequeued from thread 1: 1
Dequeued from thread 1: 2
Dequeued from thread 2: 1
Dequeued from thread 2: 2
Dequeued from thread 1: 3
```

Thread-based concurrency provides a straightforward way to execute parallel tasks. However, it requires careful synchronization when threads share data, utilizing mutexes and other synchronization primitives to ensure data consistency and avoid race conditions. By leveraging OCaml's Thread and Mutex modules, complex concurrent programs can be efficiently managed.

9.3 Parallelism with Multicore OCaml

Parallelism involves executing multiple computations simultaneously, leveraging multiple cores of a processor to perform tasks faster. Multicore OCaml allows developers to write parallel programs using shared memory, providing capabilities to efficiently utilize modern multi-core architectures.

Multicore OCaml introduces a fine-grained locking mechanism, providing parallel execution by using domain-terminated threads. A domain represents an OCaml runtime instance running on its own core, ensuring true parallelism.

Setting up Multicore OCaml involves installing a version of OCaml that supports multicore capabilities. Once you have the appropriate version, you can begin exploiting parallelism by creating and managing multiple domains. Here is an example of creating parallel tasks using Multicore OCaml:

```
(* Import the necessary modules *)
open Domain

(* A simple parallel execution task *)
let parallel_task n =
  Printf.printf "Task %d is executed by domain %d\n" n (self () |> get_id)

(* Create and join multiple domains *)
let () =
  let num_domains = 4 in
  (* Create a list of domains *)
  let domains = List.init num_domains (fun n -> spawn (fun _ -> parallel_task n)) in
  (* Join the domains *)
  List.iter join domains
```

The above code illustrates: 1. **Spawning Domains**: Using the spawn function, where each domain executes the parallel_task. 2. **Joining Domains**: Each domain is joined to ensure the main program waits for all domains to complete.

Synchronization and Shared State in Multicore OCaml can be achieved through advanced synchronization primitives. For example, Mutexes and Condition Variables are provided to manage shared resources safely.

Mutex Example:

```
open Domain
open Mutex

(* Shared counter and its associated mutex *)
let counter = ref 0
```

```
let counter_mutex = Mutex.create ()

(* Function to safely increment the counter *)
let safe_increment () =
  for _ = 1 to 1000 do
    Mutex.lock counter_mutex;
    counter := !counter + 1;
    Mutex.unlock counter_mutex;
  done

let () =
  (* Create domains to concurrently increment the counter *)
  let domains = List.init 4 (fun _ -> spawn (fun _ -> safe_increment ())) in
  List.iter join domains;
  Printf.printf "Final counter value: %d\n" !counter
```

This example demonstrates: 1. **Creating a Mutex**: To protect the shared mutable state. 2. **Locking and Unlocking**: Ensuring only one domain can modify the counter at a time.

Atomic Operations are another essential tool in parallel programming. Atomic operations can be performed without the need for complex locking mechanisms.

Atomic Counter Example:

```
open Atomic

(* Atomic counter *)
let atomic_counter = Atomic.make 0

(* Function to safely increment the atomic counter *)
let atomic_increment () =
  for _ = 1 to 1000 do
    Atomic.fetch_and_add atomic_counter 1 |> ignore
  done

let () =
  (* Create domains to concurrently increment the atomic counter *)
  let domains = List.init 4 (fun _ -> spawn (fun _ -> atomic_increment ())) in
  List.iter join domains;
  Printf.printf "Final atomic counter value: %d\n" (Atomic.get atomic_counter)
```

Advantages of using atomic operations: 1. **Reduced Overhead**: Compared to mutexes, atomic operations avoid the cost of locking. 2. **Simplicity**: Ensuring thread safety with fewer lines of code.

Multicore OCaml provides support for **Domain-local Heaps**, which reduce contention and improve efficiency by minimizing shared memory interactions. Each domain maintains its own local heap for allocation, significantly enhancing performance in memory-intensive applications.

Domain-local Heaps Example:

```
open Domain
```

```
(* Dummy function to simulate heap allocation *)
let domain_local_allocation () =
  for _ = 1 to 100000 do
    ignore (Bytes.create 1024)
  done

let () =
  (* Create domains to perform heap allocations *)
  let domains = List.init 4 (fun _ -> spawn (fun _ -> domain_local_allocation ())) in
  List.iter join domains;
  Printf.printf "Completed domain-local heap allocations.\n"
```

In practice, efficient use of domain-local heaps can lead to significant performance gains, particularly in programs with high allocation rates.

Understanding and leveraging **Parallel Algorithms** in Multicore OCaml allows developers to create high-performance applications.

Parallel Map Example:

```
open Domain

(* Parallel map function *)
let parallel_map f lst =
  let num_domains = 4 in
  let len = List.length lst in
  let chunk_size = (len + num_domains - 1) / num_domains in
  let chunks = List.init num_domains (fun i ->
    let start = i * chunk_size in
    let end_ = min len ((i + 1) * chunk_size) in
    List.sub lst start (end_ - start)
  ) in
  let tasks = List.map (fun chunk -> spawn (fun _ -> List.map f chunk)) chunks in
  List.concat (List.map join tasks)

(* Test parallel map *)
let () =
  let lst = List.init 1000 (fun x -> x) in
  let doubled_list = parallel_map (fun x -> x * 2) lst in
  Printf.printf "Doubled list head: %d\n" (List.hd doubled_list)
```

This parallel map function demonstrates: 1. **Dividing Work**: Splitting the input list into chunks for parallel processing. 2. **Combining Results**: Gathering and concatenating results from all domains.

Through these concepts and examples, Multicore OCaml equips developers with the necessary tools to fully exploit parallelism, ensuring efficient execution on multi-core processors.

9.4 Promises and Futures

Promise and future abstractions are critical concepts for managing asynchronous computations in OCaml. They provide a way to represent a value that may be available at some point in the future, allowing for non-blocking programming and better responsiveness in concurrent applications.

A promise is a writable, single-assignment container, whereas a future is a read-only view of a promise. A future represents a computation that may or may not have completed, and this completion is controlled by a promise. These abstractions decouple the production and the consumption of a value, enabling more flexible concurrency management.

First, let us consider the creation of promises and futures. In OCaml, the Lwt library provides the necessary functionality to work with these abstractions. A promise can be created using the Lwt.wait function, which returns a pair - a promise and its corresponding future.

```
#use "topfind";;
#require "lwt";;
open Lwt.Infix;;

(* Create a promise and a future *)
let (thread, wakener) = Lwt.wait ();;

(* 'thread' is the future *)
(* 'wakener' is the promise *)
```

In the code snippet above, thread is the future that will eventually hold the result of the computation, and wakener is the promise that can be used to fulfill the computation. To fulfill the promise, the Lwt.wakeup function is used.

```
(* Fulfill the promise with a value, say 42 *)
Lwt.wakeup wakener 42;;
```

Once the promise is fulfilled, the future will hold the value. Futures are typically used in conjunction with callbacks or chaining to execute actions upon the completion of the asynchronous operation.

```
(* Define a callback to execute when the future is resolved *)
thread >>= fun result ->
  Lwt_io.printf "The result is: %d\n" result
```

In this example, once the wakener is invoked with the value 42, the future thread is resolved, and the registered callback prints the result.

Promises and futures can be combined to represent more complex workflows, such as sequence of dependent computations or parallel executions. Consider the following example where two futures are combined:

```
let promise1, wakener1 = Lwt.wait ();;
let promise2, wakener2 = Lwt.wait ();;

(* Define a combined future *)
let combined_future =
  promise1 >>= fun result1 ->
  promise2 >>= fun result2 ->
  Lwt.return (result1 + result2)
;;

(* Fulfill both promises *)
Lwt.wakeup wakener1 10;;
Lwt.wakeup wakener2 32;;

(* Register a callback for the combined future *)
combined_future >>= fun combined_result ->
  Lwt_io.printf "The combined result is: %d\n" combined_result
```

Here, when both promise1 and promise2 are fulfilled, the combined future computes their sum and prints it.

Error handling is integral to working with promises and futures. The Lwt library provides mechanisms to handle exceptions within futures. If an exception occurs during the fulfillment of a promise, it can be propagated to the future using Lwt.wakeup_exn.

```
let promise, wakener = Lwt.wait ();;
let faulty_future =
  promise >>= fun _ ->
  Lwt.fail_with "Some error occurred"
;;

(* Fulfill the promise with a value initially *)
Lwt.wakeup wakener 10;;

(* Handle the error *)
Lwt.catch
  (fun () -> faulty_future)
  (fun ex ->
     Lwt_io.printf "Caught exception: %s\n" (Printexc.to_string ex))
```

In this example, when faulty_future propagates the exception, the Lwt.catch function captures it, and the provided error-handling function logs the exception.

Promises and futures in OCaml not only permit effective management of asynchronous computations but also allow for expressive and flexible handling patterns such as parallelism, sequential dependencies and error management. Applying these constructs appropriately can lead to the development of efficient and responsive concurrent applications.

9.5 Message Passing

Message passing is a fundamental concept in concurrent and parallel programming, offering a structured way for threads or processes to communicate. In OCaml, message passing enables the exchange of data between concurrent entities, facilitating coordination and data sharing while minimizing the challenges associated with shared state.

To implement message passing in OCaml, we use the Event module provided by the Thread library. This module allows us to create and manipulate events, which can be thought of as messages.

Basic Event Creation and Communication

To illustrate the fundamental concepts of message passing, we start with a simple example where one thread sends a message to another thread.

```
open Thread
open Event

let message_sender () =
  let channel = new_channel () in
  let message = "Hello from sender" in
  let sender_thread = Thread.create (fun chan -> sync (send chan message)) channel
      in
  (channel, sender_thread)

let message_receiver (channel, sender_thread) =
  let receiver_thread = Thread.create (fun chan ->
    let received_message = sync (receive chan) in
    print_endline received_message
  ) channel in
  Thread.join sender_thread;
  Thread.join receiver_thread

let main () =
  let (channel, sender_thread) = message_sender () in
  message_receiver (channel, sender_thread)

let () = main ()
```

In this example, the message_sender function creates a channel for communication and a sender thread that sends a message using the send function wrapped in the sync primitive to ensure synchronization. The message_receiver function creates a receiver thread that waits for the message with the receive function, also using sync for synchronization. The main function runs these two functions in sequence.

Bidirectional Communication

We can extend the previous example to support bidirectional communication, where two threads exchange messages. This requires two channels: one for each direction of communication.

```
open Thread
open Event

let bidirectional_sender (send_channel, receive_channel) =
  let sender_thread = Thread.create (fun (send_chan, recv_chan) ->
    sync (send send_chan "Message from sender");
    let response = sync (receive recv_chan) in
    print_endline ("Sender received: " ^ response)
  ) (send_channel, receive_channel) in
  sender_thread

let bidirectional_receiver (send_channel, receive_channel) =
  let receiver_thread = Thread.create (fun (send_chan, recv_chan) ->
    let message = sync (receive send_chan) in
    print_endline ("Receiver received: " ^ message);
    sync (send recv_chan "Acknowledgment from receiver")
  ) (send_channel, receive_channel) in
  receiver_thread

let main () =
  let send_channel = new_channel () in
  let receive_channel = new_channel () in
  let sender_thread = bidirectional_sender (send_channel, receive_channel) in
  let receiver_thread = bidirectional_receiver (send_channel, receive_channel) in
  Thread.join sender_thread;
  Thread.join receiver_thread

let () = main ()
```

This code defines two channels for sending and receiving messages in both directions. The bidirectional_sender thread sends a message and waits for a response, while the bidirectional_receiver thread waits for a message and then sends an acknowledgment. This demonstrates how message passing can be used for more complex communication patterns.

Message Passing with Multiple Threads

For scenarios involving multiple threads, OCaml's event channels can handle multiple senders and receivers, ensuring thread-safe communication.

```
open Thread
open Event

let multi_sender (send_channel, id) =
  Thread.create (fun (chan, tid) ->
    sync (send chan ("Message from thread " ^ string_of_int tid))
  ) (send_channel, id)

let multi_receiver (receive_channel, num_threads) =
```

```
  let receiver_thread = Thread.create (fun (chan, n) ->
    for _ = 1 to n do
      let message = sync (receive chan) in
      print_endline message
    done
  ) (receive_channel, num_threads) in
  receiver_thread

let main () =
  let num_threads = 5 in
  let channel = new_channel () in
  let sender_threads = Array.init num_threads (fun i -> multi_sender (channel, i)) in
  let receiver_thread = multi_receiver (channel, num_threads) in
  Array.iter Thread.join sender_threads;
  Thread.join receiver_thread

let () = main ()
```

In this example, five sender threads send messages to a single receiver thread through a common channel. The receiver thread reads and prints messages from the senders, demonstrating how message passing efficiently coordinates communication among multiple threads.

The principles of message passing offered by OCaml's Event module provide a robust foundation for concurrent programming. By using channels and events, developers can structure communication between threads clearly and safely, leveraging synchronization primitives like sync to ensure orderly and predictable message exchanges.

9.6 Shared State and Synchronization

Shared state occurs when multiple concurrent threads or processes access the same memory location. Without proper management, shared state can lead to data races, where the system's behavior becomes unpredictable due to concurrent access to shared variables. Synchronization mechanisms are necessary to control access to shared resources, ensuring data consistency and preventing race conditions.

The primary tools for synchronization in OCaml are mutexes (mutual exclusion locks), condition variables, and atomic operations. Mutexes ensure that only one thread can access a shared resource at a time. Condition variables allow threads to wait for certain conditions to be met before they proceed. Atomic operations provide a way to perform thread-safe updates to shared data without using locks, although they are generally limited to simple updates.

Mutexes

A mutex is a locking mechanism that enforces mutual exclusion in a critical section. When a thread locks a mutex, it gains exclusive access to the resource protected by that mutex. Other threads attempting to lock the same mutex will be blocked until the mutex is unlocked.

Below is an example of using mutexes in OCaml:

```
open Thread
open Mutex

let mutex = Mutex.create ()

let shared_counter = ref 0

let increment_counter () =
  Mutex.lock mutex;
  shared_counter := !shared_counter + 1;
  Mutex.unlock mutex

let () =
  let threads = List.init 10 (fun _ -> Thread.create increment_counter ()) in
  List.iter Thread.join threads;
  Printf.printf "Final counter value: %d\n" !shared_counter
```

In this example, a mutex is created using Mutex.create() and is used to ensure that only one thread can increment the shared_counter at a time. Each of the 10 threads created executes increment_counter(), where the mutex is locked before the counter is incremented and unlocked afterward.

Condition Variables

Condition variables allow threads to wait for a particular condition or signal before continuing execution. They are used in conjunction with mutexes to control the execution flow based on certain conditions.

Here is an example using condition variables:

```
open Thread
open Mutex
open Condition

let mutex = Mutex.create ()
let condition = Condition.create ()
let shared_flag = ref false

let wait_for_condition () =
  Mutex.lock mutex;
  while not !shared_flag do
    Condition.wait condition mutex
  done;
  Printf.printf "Condition met!\n";
  Mutex.unlock mutex

let signal_condition () =
  Mutex.lock mutex;
  shared_flag := true;
```

```
  Condition.signal condition;
  Mutex.unlock mutex

let () =
  let waiter_thread = Thread.create wait_for_condition () in
  Thread.delay 2.0; (* simulate some work *)
  signal_condition ();
  Thread.join waiter_thread;
```

In this example, the wait_for_condition() function waits for the shared_flag to become true. The thread will block at Condition.wait until another thread signals the condition using Condition.signal.

Atomic Operations

Atomic operations provide a means to perform thread-safe manipulations of shared data without using mutexes. The Atomic module in OCaml offers operations for integer references, such as atomic addition or exchange.

An example of using atomic operations is shown below:

```
open Thread
open Atomic

let shared_counter = Atomic.make 0

let increment_counter () =
  let rec loop () =
    let old_value = Atomic.get shared_counter in
    if not (Atomic.compare_and_set shared_counter old_value (old_value + 1))
    then loop ()
  in
  loop ()

let () =
  let threads = List.init 10 (fun _ -> Thread.create increment_counter ()) in
  List.iter Thread.join threads;
  Printf.printf "Final counter value: %d\n" (Atomic.get shared_counter)
```

In this code, the Atomic.compare_and_set function atomically compares the value of shared_counter with old_value and sets it to old_-value + 1 if they match. This operation is repeated until the increment completes successfully, ensuring that threads do not interfere with each other.

Ensuring proper synchronization is essential in concurrent programming to manage shared state effectively. By using mutexes, condition variables, and atomic operations, OCaml programs can avoid data races and ensure consistent results even in the presence of multiple threads.

9.7 Asynchronous Programming

Asynchronous programming in OCaml achieves concurrency without using traditional threads, instead employing abstractions such as promises and lightweight threads to handle operations that can proceed independently without blocking the execution of the entire program. The asynchronous model is particularly efficient for I/O-bound tasks and cooperative multitasking, where the avoidance of context switches inherent to preemptive multitasking can lead to performance improvements and simpler reasoning about code.

OCaml's primary library for asynchronous programming is the Lwt (Lightweight Thread) library. Lwt provides primitives for creating and managing promises, also referred to as deferreds, which represent values or computations that might not be immediately available.

Promises and Deferreds

A promise or deferred represents a computation that will eventually produce a value. In Lwt, this is encapsulated by the Lwt.t type. Creating and resolving promises, chaining computations, and error handling are central to working with promises.

```
(* Create an unresolved promise and its resolver *)
let (promise, resolver) = Lwt.wait ();;

(* Resolving the promise *)
Lwt.wakeup resolver "Hello, world!";;
```

Lwt.wait () creates a promise-resolver pair. The promise, promise, is initially in an unresolved state. The resolver, resolver, is used to resolve the promise with the value "Hello, world!".

Chaining Computations with Promises

Promises can be chained together using the bind function (denoted by »=), which allows sequential execution of asynchronous operations.

```
let (promise, resolver) = Lwt.wait ();;

let chain = promise >>= fun result ->
  Lwt_io.printl result >>= fun () ->
  Lwt_io.printl "Chaining promises in OCaml";;

Lwt.wakeup resolver "Hello, world!";;
Lwt_main.run chain;;
```

In this example, promise is resolved with the string "Hello, world!". The chain promise waits for promise to resolve, prints its result, and continues to print another message.

Error Handling

Handling errors in asynchronous computations follows a similar pattern to chaining. Lwt provides the catch function for handling exceptions.

```
let error_promise = Lwt.fail (Failure "An error occurred");;

let handle_error = Lwt.catch
  (fun () -> error_promise)
  (function
    | Failure msg -> Lwt_io.printl ("Caught exception: " ^ msg)
    | exn -> Lwt.fail exn
  );;

Lwt_main.run handle_error;;
```

This snippet demonstrates the catch function. When error_promise fails with a Failure exception, the error message is printed. If a different exception occurs, Lwt.fail re-raises it.

Parallel and Concurrent Execution

Asynchronous programming inherently supports running tasks concurrently. Using Lwt.join and Lwt.choose, multiple promises can be run in parallel.

```
let task1 = Lwt_io.sleep 1.0 >>= fun () -> Lwt_io.printl "Task 1 completed";;
let task2 = Lwt_io.sleep 2.0 >>= fun () -> Lwt_io.printl "Task 2 completed";;

let tasks = Lwt.join [task1; task2];;
Lwt_main.run tasks;;
```

Lwt.join waits for all the promises in the list to resolve. Here, task1 and task2 run concurrently. Despite task2 taking longer, both will execute in parallel due to the non-blocking nature of Lwt promises.

Interfacing with Synchronous Code

Integrating asynchronous code with synchronous portions of the program requires careful handling to avoid blocking the event loop. Lwt_preemptive allows running blocking functions in a separate system thread, bridged back to Lwt.

```
let blocking_function () =
  (* Simulate a blocking call *)
  Unix.sleep 3;
  "Finished Blocking Task";;

let async_wrapper () =
  Lwt_preemptive.detach blocking_function ();;

let () =
  let task = async_wrapper () >>= Lwt_io.printl in
```

```
Lwt_main.run task;;
```

Lwt_preemptive.detach offloads the blocking operation to a separate thread. Once the blocking function completes, its result is integrated back into the Lwt event loop.

Integrating these techniques provides a rich framework for efficient and maintainable async concurrency in OCaml applications. Utilizing promises and suitable asynchronous constructs enables developers to build scalable and performant systems.

9.8 Task Scheduling

Task scheduling is a fundamental aspect of implementing concurrency and parallelism in OCaml. Efficient task scheduling ensures that available computational resources are used optimally, leading to improved performance and responsiveness of concurrent programs. This section provides an in-depth analysis of task scheduling, detailing the strategies and techniques employed in OCaml for managing multiple concurrent tasks.

Task scheduling involves the management of multiple tasks or threads by allocating CPU time and arranging their execution order. In OCaml, task scheduling can be managed either by an operating system or by runtime libraries. The primary goals of task scheduling include balancing the load across multiple processors, maximizing CPU usage, minimizing response time, and managing resource contention.

Key Concepts in Task Scheduling

To understand task scheduling in OCaml, it is important to familiarize oneself with several key concepts:

- Task: The basic unit of work that is scheduled. It can be a thread, a process, or a lightweight unit of work such as a promise.
- Scheduler: The component responsible for determining the execution order of tasks. In OCaml, schedulers can be part of the runtime system or user-defined.
- Context Switching: The process of storing the state of a currently running task and restoring the state of the next task to be run. This enables multiple tasks to share a single CPU core by switching between them.

- Preemptive Scheduling: A scheduling strategy where the scheduler can interrupt a running task to allocate CPU time to another task.
- Cooperative Scheduling: A scheduling strategy where tasks voluntarily yield control of the CPU, allowing other tasks to be scheduled.

OCaml Task Scheduling Strategies

OCaml supports several strategies for task scheduling:

- Thread-Scheduler: OCaml's default runtime system includes a thread scheduler that uses preemptive multitasking.
- Lwt and Async: Libraries providing cooperative multitasking based on lightweight threads, enabling efficient asynchronous programming.
- Multicore OCaml: Introduces parallelism with domain-based task scheduling, leveraging multiple CPU cores for concurrent execution.

Thread Scheduler

OCaml's built-in thread scheduler provides basic preemptive multitasking capabilities. It uses POSIX threads (pthreads) to create and manage threads. The following example demonstrates the use of threads in OCaml:

```
(* Example of threading in OCaml *)

let thread_function () =
  for i = 1 to 5 do
    Printf.printf "Thread %d: iteration %d\n" (Thread.id (Thread.self ())) i;
    Thread.delay 0.5;
  done;;

let () =
  let t1 = Thread.create thread_function () in
  let t2 = Thread.create thread_function () in
  Thread.join t1;
  Thread.join t2;;
```

This code creates two threads, each performing five iterations, outputting their IDs and iteration counts. Thread.delay is used to simulate time consumption, allowing the scheduler to alternate between threads.

Lwt and Async Libraries

Lwt and Async are two popular libraries in OCaml for cooperative task scheduling. Both libraries provide abstractions for asynchronous programming through lightweight threads (or promises).

Lwt example:

```
(* Example of using Lwt for cooperative multitasking *)

open Lwt.Infix

let task_function () =
  Lwt_io.printf "Task started\n" >>= fun () ->
  Lwt_unix.sleep 1.0 >>= fun () ->
  Lwt_io.printf "Task finished\n";;

let () =
  let task1 = task_function () in
  let task2 = task_function () in
  Lwt_main.run (Lwt.join [task1; task2]);;
```

This example demonstrates how two Lwt tasks are created and executed. Lwt_main.run schedules the tasks cooperatively, ensuring that each task yields control while waiting for I/O operations.

Async example:

```
(* Example of using Async for cooperative multitasking *)
open Core
open Async

let task_function () =
  print_endline "Task started";
  let%bind () = after (Time.Span.of_sec 1.0) in
  print_endline "Task finished";
  return ();;

let () =
  let task1 = task_function () in
  let task2 = task_function () in
  Scheduler.go_main ~main:(fun () -> Deferred.all_unit [task1; task2]);;
```

In this example, the Async library is used to create and execute two cooperative tasks. The Scheduler.go_main function ensures that all tasks are scheduled and executed.

Multicore OCaml

Multicore OCaml introduces parallelism through the use of domains. Domains can be described as system threads capable of executing in parallel on multiple CPU cores. Task scheduling in Multicore OCaml involves distributing tasks across these domains to achieve efficient parallel execution.

Example using Domains:

```
(* Example of using Domains in Multicore OCaml *)

let domain_function () =
  Printf.printf "Hello from domain %d\n" (Domain.self () :> int);;

let () =
  let domain1 = Domain.spawn domain_function in
  let domain2 = Domain.spawn domain_function in
  Domain.join domain1;
  Domain.join domain2;;
```

This example demonstrates how to create and manage tasks across multiple domains. The Domain.spawn function creates a new domain, and Domain.join ensures synchronization by waiting for the domain's execution to complete.

Efficient task scheduling in OCaml involves understanding and utilizing appropriate scheduling strategies and libraries. The choice between preemptive and cooperative multitasking depends on the application requirements, such as the need for responsiveness or performance optimization. Furthermore, leveraging parallelism with Multicore OCaml and understanding domain-based scheduling is crucial for writing high-performance concurrent applications.

The knowledge of task scheduling directly impacts the ability to design robust and efficient concurrent applications in OCaml. As tasks grow in complexity and number, selecting the appropriate scheduling strategy and library becomes essential for maintaining performance and reliability.

9.9 Concurrency Patterns

Concurrency patterns in OCaml provide structured approaches to manage the complexity of concurrent computations effectively. There are several patterns frequently employed within OCaml to orchestrate concurrent tasks, each addressing specific types of problems related to task execution order, resource sharing, and fault tolerance.

One of the primary concurrency patterns is the **Task Queue** pattern. In this pattern, tasks are placed in a queue and processed by a predefined number of workers. This model ensures that task execution is handled asynchronously, and it is particularly useful for tasks that can run independently. In OCaml, the task queue can be implemented using a combination of threads and a mutable queue structure. The below example demonstrates a simple task queue:

```
open Thread
open Mutex

let task_queue = Queue.create ()
let queue_mutex = Mutex.create ()

let worker_thread () =
  while true do
    Mutex.lock queue_mutex;
    while Queue.is_empty task_queue do
      Mutex.unlock queue_mutex;
      Thread.yield ();
      Mutex.lock queue_mutex;
    done;
    let task = Queue.pop task_queue in
    Mutex.unlock queue_mutex;
    task ()
  done

let add_task task =
  Mutex.lock queue_mutex;
  Queue.push task task_queue;
  Mutex.unlock queue_mutex

let () =
  let workers = Array.init 4 (fun _ -> Thread.create worker_thread ()) in
  Array.iter Thread.join workers
```

In this example, worker_thread continually checks for tasks in the task_queue. The use of Mutex ensures that the shared queue is accessed safely by multiple threads, preventing data races.

Another key pattern in OCaml is the **Actor Model**. This pattern abstracts away the complexities of locking and thread management by using actors to encapsulate state and behavior. Each actor processes messages sequentially, ensuring a linear progression of execution per actor. Messages can be sent between actors, facilitating communication without shared state. The Eio library provides tools to create actors in OCaml efficiently.

Algorithm 2: Actor Model in OCaml

Data: Actors communicating via messages
Result: Sequential message processing without shared state
Input: Create an actor instance
Output: Send a message to an actor

actor_create(name: string)
for *each* message *in actor_mailbox* **do**
  | process(message)
end
actor_send(actor, message)

The **Pipeline** pattern allows for staging tasks across multiple phases which can be processed concurrently. In a pipeline, each stage performs a segment of the work and passes the processed data to the next stage. This model is efficient for data processing tasks where multiple transformations are applied in sequence. OCaml can leverage the Lwt library to implement a pipeline:

```
open Lwt.Infix

let stage_1 data =
  Lwt.return (process_stage_1 data)

let stage_2 data =
  Lwt.return (process_stage_2 data)

let stage_3 data =
  Lwt.return (process_stage_3 data)

let pipeline data =
  stage_1 data >>= stage_2 >>= stage_3
```

In the above code, stage_1, stage_2, and stage_3 represent different stages of the pipeline. The Lwt monad ensures that each stage is executed asynchronously, with the result of one stage passed to the next stage.

The **MapReduce** pattern is prevalent in processing large datasets and enables scaling computations across multiple machines or processors. In the Map phase, data is divided and processed independently, and in the Reduce phase, intermediate results are aggregated. This pattern can be implemented in OCaml using parallel execution libraries such as Parmap:

```
let map_func data =
  List.map process data

let reduce_func results =
  List.fold_left aggregate_function initial_value results

let mapreduce data =
  let intermediate_results = Parmap.parmap map_func (Parmap.L data) in
  reduce_func intermediate_results
```

In this code, map_func performs a parallel map operation on the dataset, and reduce_func combines the intermediate results. Parmap ensures that the mapping step is executed in parallel, exploiting the multicore capabilities of the hardware.

Understanding these concurrency patterns enables the efficient design and implementation of complex concurrent applications in OCaml. Each pattern offers different capabilities and trade-offs, and selecting the appropriate pattern is critical for achieving the desired performance and reliability in concurrent OCaml programs.

9.10 Debugging Concurrent Programs

Debugging concurrent programs poses unique challenges that go beyond those encountered in sequential programming due to the non-deterministic nature of concurrent execution. This section discusses strategies and tools to effectively debug concurrent programs in OCaml, emphasizing techniques to identify and resolve common concurrency issues.

The primary challenges in debugging concurrent programs include race conditions, deadlocks, and livelocks. These issues often lead to unpredictable behavior, making them difficult to reproduce and resolve. To efficiently debug these problems, it is crucial to understand their root causes and utilize appropriate debugging tools and methodologies.

Race Conditions

A race condition occurs when the behavior of a program depends on the relative timing of events, such as thread execution order, which can lead to inconsistent results. To detect and fix race conditions, consider the following approaches:

- ThreadSanitizer is a dynamic analysis tool that can detect data races in programs. Although it primarily supports C/C++ languages, similar tools are available for OCaml with varying degrees of integration.
- Employ atomic operations or synchronized constructs such as mutexes to ensure that critical sections of code are executed mutually exclusively by threads. This can prevent concurrent modification of shared resources.
- Use extensive logging to capture thread execution flow, helping to identify points where race conditions may occur. Log timestamps and thread identifiers for precise analysis.

Deadlocks

A deadlock occurs when two or more threads are unable to proceed because each is waiting for a resource held by the other. Deadlocks can halt program execution entirely. To diagnose and resolve deadlocks, use the following strategies:

- Implement a strict order in the acquisition of locks. By ensuring that all threads acquire locks in the same order, the potential for circular wait conditions is eliminated.
- Introduce timeouts for lock acquisition attempts. If a thread cannot acquire a lock within a specified timeframe, it should release any locks it holds and retry, potentially breaking the deadlock cycle.
- Utilize tools like ocamldebug to inspect thread states and the order of lock acquisitions.
- Avoid holding multiple locks simultaneously when possible, reducing the complexity of lock management.

Livelocks

A livelock occurs when threads are not blocked, but are actively attempting to resolve a conflict in a way that prevents them from making progress. To tackle livelocks, consider these practices:

- Use backoff algorithms that introduce a randomized delay before retrying actions. This can prevent threads from continuously interfering with each other.
- Monitor thread progress, and if no forward progress is detected, force threads to yield or reset their state.

Tooling and Techniques

OCaml provides various tools and techniques to support debugging of concurrent programs:

- **ocamldebug**: The OCaml debugger (ocamldebug) supports single-threaded execution debugging. Although it does not natively support multithreaded debugging, it can still be useful for inspecting the behavior of individual threads.
- **Event Trace**: Event tracing involves recording events during the execution of a program, which can later be analyzed to understand thread interactions and timing issues. Tools like LTTng or DTrace can be integrated with OCaml programs to provide this functionality.

- **Custom Logging**: Implement custom logging within your OCaml application to record significant events, thread states, and resource accesses. This helps create a timeline of operations for post-mortem analysis.
- **Deterministic Execution**: Modify your concurrent program to follow a deterministic execution path during debugging. This can be achieved by controlling thread scheduling explicitly. While it can introduce performance overhead, it simplifies the process of reproducing and diagnosing issues.

Example: Detecting and Fixing a Race Condition

Consider an example where two threads increment a shared counter variable. A race condition might occur, resulting in an incorrect final value of the counter.

```
open Thread
open Mutex

let counter = ref 0
let mutex = Mutex.create ()

let increment () =
  for _ = 1 to 1000000 do
    (* Critical section *)
    Mutex.lock mutex;
    counter := !counter + 1;
    Mutex.unlock mutex
  done

let t1 = Thread.create increment ()
let t2 = Thread.create increment ()

let () =
  Thread.join t1;
  Thread.join t2;
  Printf.printf "Final counter value: %d\n" !counter
```

In this example, the use of Mutex.lock and Mutex.unlock ensures that increments to the counter are atomic, preventing race conditions. The expected final value of counter is 2000000.

```
Final counter value: 2000000
```

This demonstrates how synchronization mechanisms can be employed to resolve concurrency issues. By thoroughly understanding these debugging techniques and utilizing the tools and methodologies outlined, one can effectively develop and maintain reliable concurrent OCaml programs.

Chapter 10

Advanced Features and Optimization

This chapter delves into advanced features and optimization techniques in OCaml, starting with metaprogramming using Ppx and macros for code generation. We will discuss interfacing with C libraries, advanced type system features, and performance profiling. Topics include memory management and optimization, manual memory management, and specific strategies for code optimization and benchmarking to enhance the performance and efficiency of OCaml programs.

10.1 Introduction to Advanced Features

OCaml, a powerful multi-paradigm programming language, offers a range of advanced features that enhance the expressiveness, flexibility, and performance of software projects. This section introduces some of these advanced capabilities, setting the stage for a deeper exploration in subsequent sections.

OCaml's advanced features can be broadly categorized into several domains:

- **Metaprogramming with Ppx**: This enables code transformation and generation at compile-time, improving abstraction and reducing boilerplate.

- **Macros and Code Generation**: Here, we delve into syntax extension and compile-time code evaluation to automate repetitive coding tasks.
- **Interfacing with C Libraries**: This discusses the bridging between OCaml and C, facilitating the use of existing C libraries and improving performance for critical sections of code.
- **Advanced Type System Features**: This covers the utilization of OCaml's sophisticated type system, including polymorphism, type inference, and GADTs (Generalized Algebraic Data Types).
- **Performance Profiling**: Methods and tools for analyzing and improving the performance of OCaml programs are discussed.
- **Memory Management and Optimization**: Techniques for managing memory efficiently in OCaml, including the garbage collector and manual memory management.
- **Manual Memory Management**: More granular control over memory allocation and deallocation is addressed here.
- **Optimization Techniques**: Strategies for optimizing OCaml code at various levels are presented.
- **Benchmarking**: Lastly, the section focuses on accurate performance measurement techniques to guide optimization efforts.

This introductory section ensures a foundational understanding of these advanced features, providing a context for their use and the benefits they offer.

Metaprogramming with Ppx allows developers to write code that generates other code, leveraging macros to reduce redundancy and improve abstraction. Ppx, or PreProcessor Extensions, powerfully transforms the abstract syntax tree (AST) of OCaml code before actual compilation. The syntax transformation can be useful for repetitive tasks, embedding domain-specific languages within OCaml, and more.

An example of a simple Ppx rewriter is shown below:

```
let reverse_list_rewriter =
  Ppxlib.Extension.V3.declare "reverse"
    Ppxlib.Extension.Context.expression
    Ppxlib.Ast_pattern.(single_expr_payload (elist __'))
    (fun ~ctxt:_ rev_list ->
```

```
let reversed_elements = List.rev rev_list in
Ppxlib.Ast_builder.Default.elist ~loc (List.map ~f:Ppxlib.Ast_builder.Default.eint
        reversed_elements))
```

Macros in OCaml allow for compile-time code generation and manipulation, making the codebase easier to maintain by reducing repetitive code blocks.

Interfacing with C Libraries bridges OCaml with low-level C programming, providing access to a vast ecosystem of libraries and enhancing performance-critical sections. The ocaml-ctypes library is particularly useful for this purpose:

```
open Ctypes
module Bindings (F : FOREIGN) = struct
  let printf = F.foreign "printf" (string @-> returning int)
end
```

The advanced type system features are amongst the most powerful aspects of OCaml. Polymorphism, higher-kinded types, and Generalized Algebraic Data Types (GADTs) are some examples. GADTs extend the expressiveness of OCaml's type system, enabling more precise type definitions and pattern matches that depend on these types. An example of a GADT in OCaml is:

```
type 'a gadt =
  | Int : int gadt
  | String : string gadt

let example : type a. a gadt -> a = function
  | Int -> 42
  | String -> "example"
```

Performance profiling in OCaml typically uses tools like gprof, perf, ocamlprof, and memprof to measure and analyze the execution of OCaml programs, identifying bottlenecks and optimization opportunities.

Memory management and optimization involve understanding the OCaml garbage collector's workings and optimizing memory usage through techniques like reducing allocation rates and using specialized data structures. Manual memory management can offer more control and is facilitated by the Bigarray and Ctypes libraries for interfacing with native memory directly.

Optimization techniques in OCaml include inlining, loop unrolling, and the use of more efficient data structures. Each technique aims to make the code faster or more memory-efficient, with benchmarks providing precise measurements of performance improvements.

Benchmarking ensures that performance optimizations are effective. Using libraries like Core_bench, developers can measure execution times accurately, comparing various implementations and guiding further optimization efforts.

This understanding offers a foundation for leveraging OCaml's advanced features effectively, ensuring high-performance, maintainable, and scalable software development.

10.2 Metaprogramming with Ppx

Metaprogramming in OCaml is a powerful technique that allows developers to write programs that generate other programs or transform existing ones. The OCaml PPX (PreProcessor eXtensions) system enables code transformation at the syntactic level before the code is compiled. Leveraging PPX for metaprogramming entails creating and utilizing custom syntax extensions to improve productivity and coding efficiency.

To comprehend PPX, it is essential to be familiar with the OCaml Abstract Syntax Tree (AST), the data structure representing OCaml code in a parsed form. PPX rewriters operate on this AST to perform syntactic transformations. Understanding the basics of AST manipulation is key to effectively leveraging PPX for metaprogramming.

Defining a Simple PPX Rewriter

Suppose we want to create a simple PPX rewriter that looks for specific patterns in the code and replaces them with more optimized equivalents. Let's start with a fundamental example that replaces a custom annotation [@optimize] with a print statement.

- Initialize a new OCaml project:

```
$ dune init project ppx_optimize
```

- Define the structure of the PPX rewriter:

```
(* file: ppx_optimize.ml *)
open Ppxlib

let optimize_mapper = object
  inherit Ppxlib.Ast_traverse.map as super

  method! expression expr =
    match expr with
    | [%expr [%optimize]] -> [%expr print_endline "Optimized"]
```

```
    | _ -> super#expression expr
end

let () =
  Driver.register_transformation ~impl:optimize_mapper "ppx_optimize"
```

This simple rewriter searches for expressions that match the specific pattern [%expr [%optimize]] and replaces them with the OCaml expression print_endline "Optimized".

- Configure the Dune build system:

```
(executable
 (name ppx_optimize)
 (libraries ppxlib))

(preprocessor_deps
 (preprocess (pps ppx_optimize)))

(env
 (dev
  (flags (:standard -open Ppx_optimize))))
```

- Compile and test the PPX rewriter:

```
$ dune build
$ dune exec -- ./ppx_optimize some_ocaml_file.ml
```

Using the PPX Rewriter in Your Project

To use the newly created PPX rewriter in an OCaml file, you would apply the [@optimize] annotation to an expression in your code:

```
(* file: some_ocaml_file.ml *)
let () =
  [%optimize]
```

Upon preprocessing and compilation, the [@optimize] annotation is transformed to print_endline "Optimized" by the PPX rewriter.

Handling Complex Transformations

While the previous example is a demonstration of simple transformation, PPX rewriters can perform far more intricate and sophisticated transformations. For instance, generating boilerplate code such as serializer and deserializer functions, deriving mathematical operations for custom types, or generating database query interfaces.

Consider a slightly more complex use case: we need to generate to_json and of_json functions for a record type. We can achieve this by defining custom attributes in our type definition and creating a PPX rewriter to generate the necessary functions.

Record definition with custom attributes:

```
type person = {
  name : string [@to_json];
  age : int [@to_json];
  address : string option [@to_json];
} [@@deriving yojson]
```

PPX rewriter implementation:

```
(* file: ppx_derived_json.ml *)
open Ppxlib
open Ast_builder.Default

let attr_str_type_decl _ctx (rec_flag, types) =
  let to_json_str =
    (* generate to_json implementation *)
    "(* to_json implementation *)"
  and of_json_str =
    (* generate of_json implementation *)
    "(* of_json implementation *)"
  in
  let str_items = [
    pstr_value Nonrecursive [
      value_binding ~pat:(patt_of_string "to_json") ~expr:(estring to_json_str);
    ];
    pstr_value Nonrecursive [
      value_binding ~pat:(patt_of_string "of_json") ~expr:(estring of_json_str);
    ];
  ] in
  [pstr_value rec_flag types] @ str_items

let () =
  Driver.register_transformation "ppx_derived_json"
    ~rules:[Context_free.Rule.(attr_str_type_decl str_type_decl)]
```

Configuration to use the PPX rewriter:

```
(preprocess
 (pps ppx_derived_json))
```

Building and testing the rewriter follows the same process as defined previously. The essence of PPX metaprogramming is leveraging syntactic transformations to inject, modify, or optimize code during the precompilation phase, pushing towards more efficient and maintainable coding practices.

Understanding and mastering PPX requires practice in manipulating AST nodes and familiarity with the OCaml compiler's internals. The transformative power it brings can significantly streamline complex code generation tasks.

10.3 Macros and Code Generation

Macros and code generation feature prominently in OCaml to facilitate the automation of repetitive coding tasks and boost productivity. Here we explore the foundational aspects of macros, their applications, and the mechanisms for automated code generation using relevant libraries and tools.

OCaml does not support traditional macros like those found in languages such as C or C++. Instead, it employs a system based on syntax extensions and code generation. A prevalent mechanism for this is through the Ppx (preprocessor extensions), which allows for compile-time code transformation and generation.

Macros Using Ppx

Ppx stands for "preprocessor extensions" and offers a robust infrastructure for defining and using macros. The Ppx system works by transforming the code before compilation, intercepting Abstract Syntax Tree (AST) representations and manipulating them accordingly.

To define a Ppx macro, one must:

1. Create the rules for AST manipulation. 2. Register these rules so that they are invoked during the preprocessing phase of compilation.

The following is a simple Ppx extension example that transforms all instances of a specific function into another for logging purposes.

```
open Ppxlib

let transform_log_function ~ctxt expr =
  match expr with
  | [%expr log(%e0)] ->
      [%expr log_with_details(filename, %e0)]
  | _ -> expr

let () =
  Driver.register_transformation
    ~rules:[ Context_free.Rule.extension
              (Extension.declare "log"
                Expression
                Ast_pattern.(single_expr_payload (pexp_ident __))
                transform_log_function ) ]
    "log_transformer"
```

In this example: - The transform_log_function function matches expressions of the form log(expr) and transforms them into log_with_details(filename, expr). - The Ppxlib.Driver.register_transformation function registers the transformation rule to be applied during preprocessing.

Code Generation

Code generation in OCaml leverages Ppx for producing code snippets automatically from metaprogramming constructs. This approach is particularly beneficial for entities like serialization functions, equality checks, and more.

Consider a case where we need to generate the boilerplate code for equality checks of a record type. Rather than writing the equality function manually, we can create a Ppx extension to automate this.

```
open Ppxlib

let generate_eq_function type_decl =
  let loc = type_decl.ptype_loc in
  match type_decl.ptype_kind with
  | Ptype_record fields ->
      let eq_expr =
        fields
        |> List.map (fun {pld_name; pld_type; _} ->
              let var_name = pld_name.txt in
              let pattern = pexp_field (evar "x") (Location.mkloc var_name loc) in
              let equality_expr = [%expr (=) [%e pattern] [%e pattern] ] in
              (Nolabel, equality_expr))
        |> pexp_tuple
      in
      [%expr fun x y -> [%e eq_expr]]
  | _ -> Location.raise_errorf ~loc
          "Equality checks are only supported for record types"

let () =
  Driver.register_transformation
    ~rules:[ Context_free.Rule.type_declaration
              (Context_free.Rule.extension
                (Extension.declare "eq"
                  Core_type (Ast_pattern.ptyp __)
                  generate_eq_function) ]
    "eq_generator"
```

In this example: - generate_eq_function takes a type declaration and constructs an equality function for record types. - The equality check function is generated by composing field-wise equality checks within the record.

Metaprogramming Benefits

Metaprogramming via macros and code generation yields several advantages:

- **Reduction of Boilerplate Code**: Automated generation of repetitive code increases productivity and consistency.
- **Enhanced Maintainability**: Code transformations encapsulate logic within well-defined macros, making the codebase easier to maintain.
- **Compile-time Safety**: Since OCaml Ppx extensions operate at compile-time, they help catch errors early, leading to safer and more robust code.

By leveraging Ppx and code generation, developers can craft more expressive and concise OCaml code, streamline development workflows, and improve code reliability. The discussed approaches demonstrate how Ppx can transform and generate code at a syntactic level, while still maintaining the functional integrity and performance optimization of OCaml programs.

10.4 Interfacing with C Libraries

Interfacing OCaml with C libraries allows developers to leverage existing C codebases, optimize performance-critical sections, and access hardware-specific features that may not be directly available in OCaml. The Foreign Function Interface (FFI) in OCaml facilitates this integration. This section will cover the following topics: preparing the build environment, writing C code for use with OCaml, creating OCaml bindings using the Ctypes library, and handling performance considerations and potential pitfalls.

To illustrate these points, we will create a simple example that calls a C function from OCaml.

Firstly, let's prepare the build environment. You will need to have a working OCaml installation and a C compiler. For this example, we will use ocamlc for compiling OCaml code and gcc for C code. Create a Makefile to automate the build process.

```
OCAMLC = ocamlc
OCAMLOPT = ocamlopt
CC = gcc
CFLAGS = -Wall -O2
LIBS = -lm
TARGET = main

all: $(TARGET)
```

```
$(TARGET): main.cmx wrapper.c
  $(CC) $(CFLAGS) -c wrapper.c
  $(OCAMLOPT) -o $(TARGET) -ccopt -L. wrapper.o main.cmx

main.cmx: main.ml
  $(OCAMLOPT) -c main.ml

clean:
  rm -f *.o *.cmi *.cmo *.cmx $(TARGET)
```

Next, we will define a simple C function in wrapper.c:

```
#include <caml/mlvalues.h>
#include <caml/alloc.h>
#include <caml/memory.h>
#include <caml/fail.h>

// Simple function that adds two integers
int add(int a, int b) {
    return a + b;
}

// OCaml wrapper for the add function
CAMLprim value ocaml_add(value a, value b) {
    CAMLparam2(a, b);
    CAMLreturn(Val_int(add(Int_val(a), Int_val(b))));
}
```

In this code, add is a simple C function that takes two integers and returns their sum. The ocaml_add function is a wrapper that converts OCaml values to C integers using the Int_val macro, calls the add function, and converts the result back to an OCaml value using Val_int.

Now, we'll provide the OCaml side of the code in main.ml:

```
(* Declare the external function *)
external add : int -> int -> int = "ocaml_add"

let () =
  let x = 3 in
  let y = 4 in
  let result = add x y in
  Printf.printf "%d + %d = %d\n" x y result
```

In main.ml, we declare the external add function, indicating that it is implemented in C and referred to as "ocaml_add". We then call this function from OCaml and print the result.

Use the provided Makefile to build and run the example:

```
$ make
$ ./main
3 + 4 = 7
```

To simplify this process, OCaml provides the Ctypes library. This library offers a more flexible and safer approach to interface with C functions directly from OCaml. Below is a revised version using Ctypes.

Modify the wrapper.c only to include the function add as follows:

```
#include <stdio.h>

// Simple function that adds two integers
int add(int a, int b) {
    return a + b;
}
```

Then, in main.ml, you can use Ctypes to define the interface:

```
open Ctypes
open Foreign

let add = foreign "add" (int @-> int @-> returning int)

let () =
  let x = 3 in
  let y = 4 in
  let result = add x y in
  Printf.printf "%d + %d = %d\n" x y result
```

Ensure that you have the Ctypes.foreign module available. This code uses Ctypes to bind the add function, which eliminates the need for writing separate wrapper functions in C. The foreign function specifies the external function signature and its name in the C library.

Rebuild the project with the appropriate libraries:

```
OCAMLC = ocamlc
OCAMLOPT = ocamlopt
CC = gcc
CFLAGS = -Wall -O2
LIBS = -lm -lctypes
TARGET = main

all: $(TARGET)

$(TARGET): wrapper.o main.cmx
  $(OCAMLOPT) -o $(TARGET) -ccopt -L. wrapper.o main.cmx -cclib -lctypes

wrapper.o: wrapper.c
  $(CC) $(CFLAGS) -c wrapper.c

main.cmx: main.ml
  $(OCAMLOPT) -package ctypes.foreign -c main.ml

clean:
  rm -f *.o *.cmi *.cmo *.cmx $(TARGET)
```

After running make and executing the application, the output remains consistent:

```
$ make
```

```
$ ./main
3 + 4 = 7
```

Integrating OCaml with C can yield performance benefits and enhance functionality by accessing mature C libraries, hardware interactions, and other system-level capabilities. Practical considerations include managing memory correctly to avoid leaks, ensuring thread-safety with appropriate synchronization, and understanding nuances of data representation.

The Ctypes library simplifies the process, reduces boilerplate code, and helps maintain safer and more readable code, particularly for complex interfaces.

10.5 Advanced Type System Features

OCaml's type system is one of its most prominent strengths, enabling powerful abstractions and ensuring type safety. In this section, we explore advanced features of OCaml's type system that enable sophisticated program design and robust error checking. We will delve into polymorphic variants, GADTs (Generalized Algebraic Data Types), first-class modules, and phantom types.

Polymorphic Variants

Polymorphic variants offer greater flexibility compared to regular variants by allowing the definition of tagged unions without predefining all possible tags. This provides an open form of variant types, facilitating extension and variation over time.

To create a basic polymorphic variant, consider the following:

```
# type color = [`Red | `Green | `Blue];;
# let string_of_color = function
    | `Red -> "Red"
    | `Green -> "Green"
    | `Blue -> "Blue";;
```

Polymorphic variants can also be combined and extended more easily:

```
# type primary = [`Red | `Green | `Blue];;
# type extended_color = [primary | `Yellow | `Cyan | `Magenta];;
```

This approach is helpful in functions where the exact type of variants might not need to be known:

```
# let blend color1 color2 = match (color1, color2) with
```

```
    | (‘Red, ‘Green) -> ‘Yellow
    | (‘Red, ‘Blue) -> ‘Magenta
    | _ -> ‘Cyan;;
```

Generalized Algebraic Data Types (GADTs)

GADTs extend the expressiveness of regular algebraic data types by allowing the specification of return type interfaces for constructors. This is remarkably useful for defining more precise types and encoding invariants directly in types.

A classic example is a typed expression evaluator:

```
type _ expr =
    | Int : int -> int expr
    | Add : int expr * int expr -> int expr
    | Bool : bool -> bool expr
    | IsZero : int expr -> bool expr

let rec eval : type a. a expr -> a = function
    | Int n -> n
    | Add (e1, e2) -> eval e1 + eval e2
    | Bool b -> b
    | IsZero e -> (eval e = 0);;
```

In the eval function, GADT constrains each expression type, ensuring that only valid expressions are evaluated.

First-Class Modules

First-class modules allow modules to be passed around like any other first-class value, providing a way to express modularity and encapsulate functionality. This is particularly powerful for designing abstractions and composing systems dynamically.

A simple implementation using first-class modules is as follows:

```
module type Comparable = sig
    type t
    val compare : t -> t -> int
end

let make_set (type a) (module M: Comparable with type t = a) =
    struct
        type t = M.t
        let empty = []
        let add x s = List.sort_uniq M.compare (x :: s)
    end
```

First-class modules can then be instantiated and used flexibly:

```
module IntCompare: Comparable with type t = int = struct
    type t = int
    let compare = Pervasives.compare
end
```

```
let int_set = make_set (module IntCompare);;
```

Phantom Types

Phantom types are types that do not have corresponding values but are used to encode additional compile-time information, enabling more granular type-safe programming constructs.

Consider an example of encoding units of measure:

```
type meter
type second
type 'a scalar = float

let time: second scalar = 9.8
let distance: meter scalar = 100.0

let speed (d: meter scalar) (t: second scalar) =
    d /. t;;
```

Here, phantom types meter and second signify different units, preventing unit mismatches during compile-time.

Understanding these advanced type system features and their practical applications not only strengthens the abstraction capabilities but also ensures robust type safety and extensibility in OCaml programs. By leveraging polymorphic variants, GADTs, first-class modules, and phantom types, we can write more expressive and error-resistant OCaml code.

10.6 Performance Profiling

Performance profiling is an essential aspect of software development that allows developers to measure and analyze various performance metrics within their programs. In OCaml, profiling provides valuable insights into the efficiency and behavior of the code, enabling developers to identify bottlenecks and optimize critical sections effectively.

Using OCaml's Native Profiling Tools

OCaml comes with a set of profiling tools that can help developers understand the performance characteristics of their programs. One of the most widely used tools is gprof, which works with programs compiled in native code. To begin profiling with gprof, you need to compile your OCaml code with the -p option. Consider the following example:

```
ocamlopt -p program.ml -o program
```

Once the program is compiled with profiling enabled, execute the program to generate a gmon.out file, which contains the profiling data.

```
./program
```

To interpret the profiling results, use gprof to analyze the gmon.out file:

```
gprof program gmon.out > analysis.txt
```

The analysis.txt file will provide detailed information about function call times, the number of calls, and the time percentage spent in each function. Here is an example of the output:

```
Flat profile:

Each sample counts as 0.01 seconds.
%    cumulative   self              self     total
time   seconds   seconds    calls  ms/call  ms/call  name
17.86     0.11     0.11       31     3.54     4.77  example_function
...
```

Heap Profiling with OCamlPro's memprof

In addition to CPU profiling, memory management is a critical aspect of performance analysis. OCamlPro's memprof is a tool specifically designed for heap profiling in OCaml programs. It can help identify memory usage patterns and detect memory leaks. To use memprof, follow these steps:

- Install memprof via OPAM:

```
opam install memprof
```

- Compile your OCaml program with the -runtime-variant option:

```
ocamlopt -runtime-variant p program.ml -o program
```

- Execute your program to generate memory profiling data:

```
OCAMLRUNPARAM='p' ./program
```

The output will contain detailed memory usage statistics, which can be analyzed to optimize memory-intensive segments of your code.

Instrumenting Code for Profiling

Another effective method for performance profiling in OCaml is manual instrumentation of the code. This involves adding specific profiling code to your program to measure execution times of critical sections. The Unix module provides useful functions for this purpose. For instance, consider the following example:

```
let time_function f x =
  let start_time = Unix.gettimeofday () in
  let result = f x in
  let end_time = Unix.gettimeofday () in
  Printf.printf "Execution time: %f seconds\n" (end_time -. start_time);
  result

let example_function n =
  (* Function implementation goes here *)
  n

let () =
  let _ = time_function example_function 42 in
  ()
```

This code snippet wraps the execution of example_function with timing code to measure and print the execution duration.

Using ocamlprof

ocamlprof is another profiling tool that provides information about how often each part of your program is executed. To use ocamlprof, first compile your code with the -p option:

```
ocamlc -p program.ml -o program
```

Run the program to collect profiling data and then use ocamlprof to annotate the source code with execution counts:

```
./program
ocamlprof program.ml > annotated_program.ml
```

Opening the annotated_program.ml file reveals line-by-line execution counts, providing insight into which parts of the code are executed most frequently. This information can illuminate performance hotspots for further optimization.

By leveraging these profiling tools and techniques, OCaml developers can gain a nuanced understanding of their application's performance characteristics and make informed decisions to enhance computational efficiency and resource utilization.

10.7 Memory Management and Optimization

Memory management in OCaml is facilitated primarily through its garbage collection mechanism, which is a powerful but intricate system. OCaml uses a generational garbage collector to manage memory. This garbage collector is divided into two generations: the minor heap and the major heap. Understanding these concepts is critical to optimizing OCaml programs for both performance and memory efficiency.

OCaml's memory model consists of the minor heap for short-lived objects and the major heap for long-lived objects. New objects are first allocated in the minor heap; when this heap is exhausted, a minor collection is triggered. During a minor collection, surviving objects are promoted to the major heap.

A core idea for optimization is reducing the frequency of garbage collection events, particularly minor collections, since these can momentarily halt program execution.

```
let rec create_list n acc =
  if n <= 0 then acc
  else create_list (n - 1) (n :: acc)
```

The above example demonstrates a pattern that may cause frequent allocations. Here, the create_list function continually allocates new cons cells in the minor heap. Optimizing this function involves minimizing allocations, possibly by preallocating storage or reusing existing data structures.

Major Collections: The major heap uses a mark-and-sweep collector. To optimize for major collections, it's essential to control the growth of long-lived objects, utilize weak references judiciously, and manage external resources efficiently.

Efficient use of data structures is another critical aspect. For instance, choosing between arrays and lists can have a significant impact. Lists are preferable for sequences with frequent addition and removal, assuming list head operations. Conversely, arrays offer constant-time access and are more space-efficient for indexed collections.

```
let array_example () =
  let arr = Array.make 1000 0 in
  for i = 0 to 999 do
    arr.(i) <- i
  done;
  arr
```

The array_example function demonstrates an efficient use of arrays. Here, both the allocation and update of array elements are performed in constant time.

Handling Immutable Data: OCaml's widespread use of immutable data structures implies frequent allocations. Utilizing Obj.magic for casting or mutable types when appropriate can sometimes reduce this, but at the cost of breaking immutability safety guarantees.

Foreign Function Interface (FFI): Control OCaml memory from C-code when interfacing with C libraries. Managing memory in C may require explicit deallocation. In OCaml, you can manage such pointers using Ctypes or similar bindings.

Example of interfacing OCaml with C using Ctypes:

```
(* Simple example using Ctypes to interface OCaml and C *)
open Ctypes
open Foreign

let malloc = foreign "malloc" (int @-> returning (ptr void))
let free = foreign "free" (ptr void @-> returning void)

let () =
  let memory = malloc 1024 in
  (* Use the memory... *)
  free memory
```

Optimization Strategies: Profiling tools such as ocamlprof and gprof can identify hotspots and help optimize code performance. Aggressive inlining ('@inline' attribute) and leveraging unboxed types can reduce overhead but should be balanced against code size and clarity.

Example of inlining a function:

```
[@@@ocaml.inline always]
let add x y = x + y
```

The [@@@ocaml.inline always] directive forces the compiler to inline the add function, reducing the function call overhead.

Using linear data access patterns improves cache locality, hence, performance. Loop unrolling and loop fusion can similarly enhance efficiency—reducing the number of iterations or combining loops to minimize overhead.

Memory Allocation Patterns: Careful management of allocation patterns minimizes the number of cache misses and page faults, both costly operations. Allocate objects likely to be used together consecutively, improving spatial locality.

Threading and Concurrency: OCaml's garbage collector is optimized for single-threaded workloads. Multithreading introduces complexity, requiring careful synchronization to avoid performance degradation. Using domain-specific concurrency libraries like Lwt and Async can manage these complexities, offering efficient I/O operations with cooperative threading.

```
open Lwt.Infix

let fetch_url url =
  Cohttp_lwt_unix.Client.get (Uri.of_string url) >>= fun (resp, body) ->
  let code = resp |> Cohttp.Response.status |> Cohttp.Code.code_of_status in
  Lwt.return code
```

In this example, Lwt provides concurrency-related functions enabling non-blocking I/O operations, promoting efficient use of system resources.

A holistic approach to memory management and optimization involves a combination of profiling, understanding of OCaml's internal mechanisms, prudent use of data structures, and minimizing unnecessary allocations, all while leveraging OCaml's abstractions and FFI capabilities. By integrating these strategies, the performance and memory efficiency of OCaml programs can be significantly improved.

10.8 Manual Memory Management

In OCaml, memory management is predominantly handled by the garbage collector, which alleviates programmers from the cumbersome task of manual memory deallocation. However, there are scenarios where manual memory management could be advantageous, particularly in interfacing with C libraries or optimizing critical sections of the code to reduce the overhead introduced by automatic memory management.

When dealing with manual memory management, OCaml provides several mechanisms and interfaces to allocate and deallocate memory explicitly. Essential functions for manual memory management include alloc, malloc, free, and Gc.compact. Below, we present detailed explanations and code examples to illustrate these functions and their uses.

```
(* Allocate an array of 10 integers *)
let size = 10
let int_array = Array.make size 0
```

In the above example, an array of ten integers is allocated using Array.make. While this is still managed by the garbage collector, it sets the ground for more advanced techniques where different allocation patterns are necessary.

```
open Bigarray

(* Allocate a big array of floats *)
let big_float_array = Array1.create float64 c_layout size

(* Access and modify elements *)
Array1.set big_float_array 0 3.14
let value = Array1.get big_float_array 0
```

The Bigarray module enables the handling of large numerical arrays that are often essential for scientific computing and interfacing with C code efficiently. The Array1.create function explicitly allocates an array suitable for manipulation in both OCaml and C.

```
open Ctypes
open Foreign

(* Define and allocate a structure manually *)
let my_struct = structure "my_struct"
let field1 = field my_struct "field1" int
let field2 = field my_struct "field2" float
let () = seal my_struct

(* Allocate memory for structure *)
let mem = allocate my_struct { field1 = 0; field2 = 0.0 }
```

Using the Ctypes module, you can directly allocate and manipulate memory with structures defined in the C language. The allocate function reserves memory for the structure, which contains an integer field and a float field in the above example.

```
open Ctypes
open Foreign

(* Wrapping C standard library functions *)
let malloc = foreign "malloc" (size_t @-> returning (ptr void))
let free = foreign "free" (ptr void @-> returning void)

(* Allocate and free memory manually using C functions *)
let manual_alloc size =
  let ptr = malloc (Unsigned.Size_t.of_int size) in
  (* Perform operations using ptr *)
  free ptr
```

The code demonstrates how to wrap standard memory management functions from the C library using the Ctypes and Foreign modules. The malloc function allocates a specified amount of memory, and the free function deallocates that memory, preventing memory leaks.

```
let perform_allocation size =
  let rec loop n =
    if n > size then
      Gc.compact () (* Triggering manual garbage collection *)
    else
      let _ = allocate_n int ~count:n in loop (n + 1)
  in
  loop 0

let () = perform_allocation 1_000_000
```

While manually managing memory can lead to performance gains, it is crucial to consider triggering garbage collection (GC) manually using Gc.compact at appropriate intervals to optimize memory usage and application performance. In scenarios with extensive, fine-grained allocations, calling the garbage collector strategically can balance memory consumption without burdening the automatic memory manager excessively.

By comprehending and using these memory management strategies judiciously, programmers can achieve refined control over the memory lifecycle in their applications, leading to optimized performance and resource utilization.

10.9 Optimization Techniques

Optimization is an essential aspect of programming that aims to improve the performance and efficiency of the code. In the context of OCaml, various optimization techniques can be employed to achieve better resource utilization, faster execution times, and enhanced overall performance. This section covers several optimization strategies, including algorithmic optimizations, data structure optimizations, and low-level code optimizations specific to OCaml.

Algorithmic Optimizations

The choice of algorithm can have a significant impact on the performance of a program. It is crucial to select algorithms that are optimal for the specific problem at hand, considering factors such as time complexity and space complexity. Here is an example of optimizing a sorting algorithm:

```
(* Inefficient bubble sort implementation *)
let bubble_sort lst =
  let len = List.length lst in
  let rec sort = function
    | 0 -> lst
```

```
  | n ->
    let lst = ref lst in
    for i = 0 to n - 2 do
      if List.nth !lst i > List.nth !lst (i + 1) then
        let temp = List.nth !lst i in
        lst := List.mapi (fun j x -> if j = i then List.nth !lst (i + 1) else if j = i + 1
              then temp else x) !lst
      done;
    done;
    sort (n - 1)
in
sort len
```

```
(* Efficient quicksort implementation *)
let rec quicksort = function
| [] -> []
| pivot::rest ->
  let left, right = List.partition ((>=) pivot) rest in
  quicksort left @ [pivot] @ quicksort right
```

quicksort is generally more efficient compared to bubble_sort due to its lower average-case time complexity, exemplifying how algorithmic choices can impact performance.

Data Structure Optimizations

Choosing appropriate data structures is vital for optimizing the performance of OCaml programs. OCaml provides various built-in data structures such as lists, arrays, and maps that can be used based on specific requirements:

```
(* Using lists for simple stack operations *)
let stack_push stack x = x :: stack

let stack_pop = function
| [] -> raise (Invalid_argument "Empty stack")
| x::xs -> (x, xs)
```

However, lists are not always the best choice due to their linear time complexity for index-based access. Arrays can provide more efficient element access and update times:

```
(* Using arrays for efficient random access *)
let array_push arr x =
  let new_arr = Array.append arr [| x |] in
  new_arr

let array_pop arr =
  let len = Array.length arr in
  if len = 0 then raise (Invalid_argument "Empty array") else
  (arr.(len - 1), Array.sub arr 0 (len - 1))
```

Using more efficient data structures can greatly reduce execution time and memory usage.

Low-Level Code Optimizations

Low-level optimizations involve fine-tuning the code to exploit specific language features and compiler optimizations. For instance, avoiding unnecessary allocation and using tail recursion can lead to significant performance gains:

```
(* Avoiding unnecessary allocation *)
let rec fib n =
  match n with
  | 0 -> 0
  | 1 -> 1
  | n -> fib (n - 1) + fib (n - 2)
```

The above implementation of Fibonacci numbers involves redundant recursive calls. A more optimized approach is to use tail recursion:

```
(* Efficient tail-recursive Fibonacci implementation *)
let fib n =
  let rec aux n a b =
    match n with
    | 0 -> a
    | _ -> aux (n - 1) b (a + b)
  in
  aux n 0 1
```

Tail recursion ensures that the recursive call is the last operation in the function, allowing the compiler to optimize and reuse the current stack frame, which conserves memory and prevents stack overflow.

Inline Functions and Unrolling Loops

Inlining functions can also reduce function call overhead. Although OCaml's compiler performs automatic inlining, explicitly guiding it by using the [@@inline] attribute can further optimize performance:

```
(* Example of inlining a function *)
let[@inline] square x = x * x

let result = square 5
```

Unrolling loops can reduce loop control overhead, though this should be done cautiously as it may increase code size.

Benchmarking and Profiling

To ensure improvements, it is essential to benchmark and profile the code before and after optimization. OCaml provides tools such as ocamlprof and libraries like Bench for this purpose:

```
#require "core_bench"

open Core_bench.Std
```

```
let naive_fib n =
  let rec fib n =
    match n with
    | 0 -> 0
    | 1 -> 1
    | n -> fib (n - 1) + fib (n - 2)
  in
  fib n

let optimized_fib n =
  let rec aux n a b =
    match n with
    | 0 -> a
    | _ -> aux (n - 1) b (a + b)
  in
  aux n 0 1

let () =
  let tests = [ Bench.Test.create ~name:"Naive Fib" (fun () -> ignore (naive_fib 20));
                Bench.Test.create ~name:"Optimized Fib" (fun () -> ignore (
                      optimized_fib 20)) ] in
  Bench.make_command tests |> Command.run
```

```
Estimated testing time 20s (2 benchmarks x 10s).

  Name            Time/Run      mWd/Run     mjWd/Run

  Naive Fib       5.176ms     78767.78     4.192
  Optimized Fib    11.00ns        6.00     0.00
```

By assessing the runtime characteristics, we can focus on the sections of code that are the bottleneck and ensure the effectiveness of our optimizations.

Optimizing OCaml programs involves employing higher-level algorithmic and data structure strategies, fine-tuning low-level code specifics, and rigorously benchmarking and profiling to verify improvements. Through these combined approaches, one can achieve substantial advancements in performance and efficiency.

10.10 Benchmarking

Benchmarking is a critical process in software development that involves measuring the runtime performance and resource usage of code to identify bottlenecks and areas for improvement. In OCaml, benchmarking typically focuses on execution time, memory usage, and other performance metrics to ensure that programs are both efficient and scalable.

To begin with benchmarking in OCaml, one must understand the essential tools and libraries available. The most commonly used library for benchmarking in OCaml is Core_bench. This library provides a robust framework for micro-benchmarking, allowing developers to measure the performance of small code snippets accurately.

Installing Core_bench: To benchmark code with Core_bench, it is necessary to have the library installed. This can be achieved via OPAM, the OCaml package manager, using the following command:

```
$ opam install core_bench
```

Creating a Benchmark: Creating a benchmark involves writing a program that uses Core_bench to measure the performance of specific functions. Below is an example benchmark that compares the performance of two different implementations of a function that calculates the sum of the first n integers.

```
open Core
open Core_bench

let rec sum_recursive n =
  if n <= 0 then 0
  else n + sum_recursive (n - 1)

let sum_iterative n =
  let rec loop acc n =
    if n <= 0 then acc
    else loop (acc + n) (n - 1)
  in
  loop 0 n

let benchmarks = [
  Bench.Test.create ~name:"sum_recursive"
    (fun () -> ignore (sum_recursive 1000));
  Bench.Test.create ~name:"sum_iterative"
    (fun () -> ignore (sum_iterative 1000));
]

let () =
  Command.run (Bench.make_command benchmarks)
```

In this example, two functions, sum_recursive and sum_iterative, are defined to calculate the sum of the first 1000 integers. The Bench.Test.create function creates benchmark tests for these two functions. The Bench.make_command function is then used to run these benchmarks.

Running the Benchmark: To execute the benchmark, compile the OCaml code and run the resulting executable. Assuming the code is saved in a file named benchmark.ml, use the following commands:

```
$ ocamlfind opt -linkpkg -package core_bench benchmark.ml -o benchmark
$ ./benchmark
```

Upon running the executable, Core_bench will produce output similar to the following:

```
Name            Time/Run   Percentage
-----------------------------------
sum_recursive  1.23us        50.0%
sum_iterative  1.23us        50.0%
```

This output provides a clear comparison of the execution times of the two functions, allowing for easy identification of the more efficient implementation. Note that the times are given in microseconds.

Analyzing the Results: The results from Core_bench provide insights into which function performs better under the tested conditions. Alongside raw execution time, Core_bench can also display various statistical metrics such as mean, median, and standard deviation. This detailed information is crucial for making informed decisions about code optimizations.

Advanced Benchmarking Techniques: Beyond basic benchmarking, Core_bench supports more advanced techniques to analyze code performance under different conditions:

- Parametric Benchmarks - It allows varying parameters to study the performance impact. For instance, varying the size of input data to see the scaling behavior of algorithms.

```
open Core
open Core_bench

let sum_iterative n =
  let rec loop acc n =
    if n <= 0 then acc
    else loop (acc + n) (n - 1)
  in
  loop 0 n

let benchmarks = Bench.Test.create_indexed
  ~name:"sum_iterative"
  ~args:[100; 1000; 10000]
  (fun n -> fun () -> ignore (sum_iterative n))

let () =
  Command.run (Bench.make_command [benchmarks])
```

- Memory Usage - Core_bench extension Gg_Profiler can be used to profile memory allocations and garbage collection metrics.

- Profiling - Coupling benchmarking with profiling tools (such as ocamlprof, perf) provides deeper insights into where the most time is spent or which parts of code are most resource-intensive.

The process of benchmarking efficiently integrates with profiling, memory analysis, and other optimization techniques. It provides granular performance metrics, paving the way for performance improvements and ensuring optimized utilization of resources in OCaml applications.

Made in United States
North Haven, CT
10 November 2026

22091354R00143